# Victorian Parables

# CONTINUUM *NEW DIRECTIONS IN RELIGION AND LITERATURE*

This series aims to showcase new work at the forefront of religion and literature through short studies written by leading and rising scholars in the field. Books will pursue a variety of theoretical approaches as they engage with writing from different religious and literary traditions. Collectively, the series will offer a timely critical intervention to the interdisciplinary crossover between religion and literature, speaking to wider contemporary interests and mapping out new directions for the field in the early twenty-first century.

*Blake. Wordsworth. Religion.* Jonathan Roberts
*Do the Gods Wear Capes?* Ben Saunders
*England's Secular Scripture,* Jo Carruthers
*Late Walter Benjamin,* John Schad
*The New Atheist Novel,* Arthur Bradley and Andrew Tate

**Forthcoming:**

*Glyph and the Gramophone,* Luke Ferretter

# Victorian Parables

*Susan E. Colón*

New Directions in Religion and Literature

continuum

Continuum International Publishing Group
The Tower Building          80 Maiden Lane
11 York Road                Suite 704
London                      New York
SE1 7NX                     NY 10038

www.continuumbooks.com

© Susan E. Colón 2012

All rights reserved. No part of this publication may be reproduced or transmitted in any form or by any means, electronic or mechanical, including photocopying, recording, or any information storage or retrieval system, without prior permission in writing from the publishers.

The author has asserted his/her right under the Copyright, Designs and Patents Act, 1988, to be identified as Author of this work.

**British Library Cataloguing-in-Publication Data**
A catalogue record for this book is available from the British Library.

ISBN: PB: 978-1-4411-4650-2
HB: 978-0-8264-4348-9

**Library of Congress Cataloging-in-Publication Data**
Colón, Susan E.
 Victorian parables / Susan E. Colon.
 p. cm. – (New directions in religion & literature)
 Includes bibliographical references and index.
 ISBN 978-1-4411-4650-2 (pbk.) – ISBN 978-0-8264-4348-9 (hardcover)
 1. English fiction–19th century–History and criticism. 2. Parables in literature.
 3. Christianity and literature–England–History–19th century.
 4. Christianity in literature. I. Title. II. Series.
 PR878.R5C65 2012
 823'.809–dc23
 2011028609

Typeset by Deanta Global Publishing Services, Chennai, India

*For Larry and Becky Burrow*

# CONTENTS

*Preface* viii

1  Parable as Literature, Literature as Parable  1

2  The Extraordinary in the Ordinary: Parable and Realism  23

3  "The Parable of Actual Life": Charlotte Yonge's *The Heir of Redclyffe*  41

4  Prodigal Sons in the Fiction of Margaret Oliphant  63

5  "The Agent of a Superior": Stewardship Parables in *Our Mutual Friend*  93

*Afterword* 121
*Notes* 123
*Bibliography* 139
*Index* 153

# PREFACE

*Victorian Parables* makes a two-fold intervention: on the side of religion-and-literature studies generally and on the side of Victorian studies particularly. As a book about religion and literature, *Victorian Parables* reexamines the critical history on biblical parables and extrabiblical parables in order to theorize how extrabiblical texts both imitate and transform the parable genre. In spite of the vast literature on parables in diverse exegetical, theological, and literary–critical modes of approach, this project has rarely been attempted and, I think, never achieved. When biblical or theological scholars attempt to apply their studies of parables to literature, they typically fail to appreciate elements of literary history and critical theory with which professional literary criticism is engaged. By the same token, when literary scholars call on the parable genre to help them interpret a work of literature, they typically do so informed by only the most rudimentary understanding of the nature and effect of parables and their place in the Jewish and Christian traditions. To many literary critics, parable is roughly synonymous with fable or illustrative tale or even allegory: a story that makes a point, usually a moral point, about the world outside the story. To some, it indicates a vaguely Christian sensibility; to others, it more truly indicates defiance of the Christian tradition. Theologians who understand better the specific performative and confrontational elements of parables do not usually translate this understanding effectively into literary analysis that is sensitive to historical or critical contexts of the texts under consideration. Moreover, they understandably find only the most conspicuous examples of extrabiblical parables which self-advertise as such. These two groups, theologians and literary critics, share the common topic of parables, but they have not found a common language, and each produces studies relatively uninformed by the insights of the other. *Victorian Parables* brings these discourses together to construct and then to deploy a theoretical framework for approaching extrabiblical parables that is precise enough to be meaningful and expansive enough to comprehend the wide variety of literary engagements with parables. In particular, I find in narratology the basis for the common language that has been lacking. The distinctive quality of parables, as I will show, is the use of plot to stage a gap, often disorienting in nature, between ordinary human life and transformed, perfected human life. The apprehension of this gap becomes an invitation to the reader to place him- or herself on one side or the other.

In the first chapter, I sift through the history of parable interpretation, and the accompanying attempts to extend that interpretation to the reading of literature, with the aim of clarifying the importance and the difficulties of generating a critical discourse that does justice to the paradoxes of parable. Critical history reveals a persistent yet crippling tendency for scholars to emphasize the parables' propositional message at the expense of their literary form, or their performativity at the expense of their moral claims, or their inconclusivity at the expense of their affirmation, or their resistance to religious constructs at the expense of their formative place in those same religious constructs. Appealing to Paul Ricoeur's theory of parable as the most successful in negotiating these paradoxes, I suggest how that theory could ground a study of extrabiblical parables. Ricoeur shows that parables are narratives that depict the extraordinary in the ordinary; the presence of an extravagant reversal in the plot is the occasion for a redescription of human experience as "limit-experience," or perfected human life. Extrabiblical parables, then, are narratives that depict or suggest a transformed human existence through the use of plotted reversals that confront the reader's conventional moral assumptions. Since the reversals of the canonical parables are so well known as to be commonplace, extrabiblical parables may undertake to renew their startling effect by plotting double reversals. It is hoped that the theory mapped in this chapter may be helpful to scholars interested in the presence of parabolic dimensions of texts in any literary period in any locale influenced by the Hebrew and Christian scriptures.

For the remainder of the book, I turn to the application of this theory to my own area of specialization, Victorian Britain, and that period's preeminent fictional form, realism. My second chapter disputes the traditional assumption that realism and parable are mutually incompatible. Not only is this exclusion unwarranted, given the dependence of biblical parables on mimetic storytelling, but it is also untrue to the best insights of recent research on Victorian realism. That research complicates the older notion of realism as epistemologically self-assured and reassuring with a view of the genre as committed to earnest but skeptical examination of epistemological as well as ethical assumptions. Such examination is held by some to be inherently and necessarily secular, but I suggest that the parables provide a window on a mode of narrative that makes possible the expression of a Christian view of life in "secular," everyday realities. What has been said of Jesus as a parabolist is equally true of the realist writers I will be considering: "Jesus, without saying so, by his very way of presenting man, shows that for him man's destiny is at stake in his ordinary creaturely existence – domestic, economic, and social" (Wilder, *Early Christian Rhetoric* 74). Thus realism's focus on probability and material particularity is no bar to the genre's participation in a Christian worldview.

Chapters three through five illustrate these claims with readings of three novels from the 1850s and 1860s. The first, Charlotte M. Yonge's *The Heir of Redclyffe* (1853), offers a prime example of my theory of parable applied to realist fiction. In this novel, Yonge retells the parable of the Pharisee and the publican in such a way as to retain the parable's countercultural and confrontational effect. Yonge, an ardent adherent of the Oxford Movement, does so in keeping with the Tractarian doctrine of reserve which saw parables as an originary instance of divine reserve in communicating religious knowledge. The novel is finally not only exemplary but also performative and perlocutionary in the manner of Jesus's parables. That is to say, it not only offers the reader a model to imitate, but it also provokes a reaction in the reader to the radical claim that the vicious and despised hypocrite can, through repentance, receive the favor of God. The reactions of readers in our time no less than in Yonge's show that it is hard to be neutral about that claim. Chapter four considers Margaret Oliphant's recurring appropriation of the parable of the prodigal son, with a particular focus on *The Perpetual Curate* (1864). Oliphant's treatment of this parable here and in other fictional and autobiographical texts shows a tendency to desentimentalize the parable in comparison with other contemporaneous treatments. However, Oliphant's bracing refusal to accept the platitudinous consolations which the Victorians usually read into the parable does not constitute a rejection of its authority or of its hopefulness. Rather, the parable becomes for her a way to think through painful and persistent questions about divine justice and human suffering. The final chapter examines Charles Dickens's *Our Mutual Friend* (1865) in terms of its engagement with Jesus's parables of stewardship. As the multiple interrelated plots of Dickens's last completed novel play out variations on the theme of stewardship, Dickens indicates that the posture of stewardship enables one to accumulate and hold wealth and power without undergoing moral degradation. In each of these texts, one or more synoptic parables provide not just a set of background allusions to guide the reader's understanding of the story and characters, but also a narrative form and strategy that achieves a genuine confrontation with Victorian sensibilities.

These chapters contest a number of explicit and implicit critical assumptions that prevail in both religious and literary studies. In addition to establishing the compatibility of realism and parable to which I have already referred, *Victorian Parables* corrects the strange omission of literary works *within* the Christian tradition from discussions of parables in literature. As we will see below, influential scholars of parables in literature have ignored or denied the possibility that worthy extrabiblical parables can be found in literary works by Christians. The authors under consideration here show notable religious differences and have different relationships to the Christian tradition, and those particularities will be given their full due. Nevertheless, all of these authors are identifiable as Christians, and their appropriations and reinscriptions of the parables mostly lie with the grain of the biblical text, though they are also hermeneutically innovative.

In terms of Victorian studies, *Victorian Parables* participates in both the ethical turn and the religious turn (though more fully in the latter than the former), and this combination is itself significant. In some quarters, it seems that ethics has been allowed back into the literary–critical conversation on the condition that it is divorced from religion; at the same time, the growing number of studies on Victorian religion in literature have tended to leave ethics out of view. Of course, studies of ethics in literature and of religion in literature can be – and have been – of immense value in themselves, but given the very strong overlap between these two domains in the Victorian period, some willingness for today's Victorianists to cross these disciplinary boundaries would seem to be important and fruitful. In this study, questions of how texts construct ethical relationships with readers are inseparable from questions of how biblical forms and tropes are reinscribed into Victorian literary contexts. In the novels I examine, as in the synoptic parables, narrative puts the theological and the ethical in productive tension. Moreover, the distinctive character of an author's narrative interpretation of a parable can only be clearly seen in light of other standard homiletic and theological interpretations prevalent at the time. My chapters will thus engage these novels from multiple angles of vision, illuminating their formal achievements as well as their social, ethical and theological commentary, all of which are implicated in each other.

\* \* \* \* \*

I am undoubtedly among those to whom much has been given. My institution and my colleagues at Baylor have given me support and encouragement without which I and my writing would be much the poorer. Some of them, including David Jeffrey, Phil Donnelly, Ralph Wood, Barry Harvey, Peaches Henry, and Alisha Barker, have read drafts of this material thoughtfully and critically. Others of them, including Josh King, Lynne Hinojosa, Andy Wisely, and Bruce Longenecker, have patiently and responsively listened to the thoughts I was trying to put on paper. A semester sabbatical awarded by Baylor University supported my completion of the project. More than all these particular kindnesses, however, I am immensely gifted simply by being part of Baylor's Honors College, where I and my colleagues from different disciplines jointly pursue the call to truth, beauty, and goodness. As cheerful as they are generous, as peaceable as they are truthful, they have taught me each in her or his way to think across disciplinary lines to enrich my thinking, teaching, writing and living. My students, too, continually give me the gift of their attention, trust, and fresh lines of thought as we participate in the age-old conversation with the great texts that undergird humanistic inquiry, and their enthusiasm gives me energy for projects such as this one.

Portions of this book have been previously disseminated, and I am grateful to the editors and audiences involved for their help in its development. Audiences and respondents at the North American Victorian Studies Association, the Victorian Institute, the Victorian Studies Association of the Western United States, and the Southeastern Conference on Christianity and Literature offered helpful insights on my work in progress. Chapter three appeared as "Realism and Parable in Charlotte Yonge's *The Heir of Redclyffe*" in *Journal of Narrative Theory* 40.1 (2010): 29–52. Series editors Mark Knight and Emma Mason have given careful attention and astute response to each page of this volume, always accompanied by gracious encouragement. Continuum's series in New Directions in Religion and Literature is itself a welcome gift of opportunity for this project, which is grounded in Victorian studies but the ambitions and implications of which extend outside of that discipline.

The gifts from my husband, Carlos Colón, and my daughters, Elise and Monica, are precious beyond description. Their love is borne unto me daily in gestures great and small. This book is dedicated to my parents, Larry and Becky Burrow, whose gifts of tender love and profound wisdom arise from nothing less than the extravagance of the gospel itself.

# 1
# Parable as Literature, Literature as Parable

When Frances Power Cobbe challenged the Evangelical emphasis on the doctrine of the atonement of Christ, she wrote that

> It would be instructive to consider what the Parable of the Prodigal *ought* to have been on the hypothesis that Christ taught the doctrine of His own Mediation in the popular [Evangelical] sense. Without irreverence – rather with the profoundest reverence for the holiest words in the holiest of books – may we not suggest that, *if they had been meant to teach the Atonement –* nay, to leave room for a Doctrine of Atonement – they must have been changed from their sublime descriptions of simple, Fatherly love, to words on this wise:
> 
> 'And when he was yet a great way off, his Elder Brother met him:
> 
> 'And he fell down at his feet and said: O my brother, entreat the Father for me; for thou art his well-beloved Son, and all that thou sayest unto him he will do.'
> 
> 'Then the elder brother had compassion on his younger brother, and went in unto his Father, and said unto him: O my Father, thou knowest that I am always with thee, neither disobeyed I thy commandments at any time, but was obedient unto death, even the death of the cross. Therefore for my sake forgive my brother, and turn away thy fierce anger against him, and blot out his transgressions.'
> 
> 'Then the Father hearkened unto his Elder Son, and was entreated for his younger son, and forgave him, and suffered him to dwell in his house.

'And the younger son feared his Father all his days, and was obedient unto him.

'But he loved his elder brother greatly, and called himself by his name.' (*Broken Lights* 49, emphasis in original)

Cobbe's reverent yet transgressive reinscription of the parable of the prodigal son captures many of the tensions and fissures characteristic to Victorian appropriations of Jesus's parables. Cobbe's use of the biblical text is simultaneously allusive and transformative. Cobbe assumes that her audience knows the parable of Luke 15, not only in its general outline but also in its details and even phrasing. The evident transgressiveness of Cobbe's retelling is subdued by her framing it as a counter-actual version: what the parable would have to be if Evangelical soteriology were found in the teaching of Jesus. The parable, as it actually stands in Luke, remains for Cobbe the authoritative as well as the appealing one – the one, in fact, that Cobbe claims is neglected by her Evangelical opponents. Nevertheless, Cobbe does not hesitate here and elsewhere to appropriate parables and other biblical forms and phrases for her own ends.[1] In particular, even while denying authority to her revision, Cobbe posits an interpretative norm for the original version. By claiming that the parable would have to be different if the doctrine of the atonement were true, she implies a particular way of reading the parable, namely, as a story illustrating the workings of salvation.[2] Turning the parable into a tale that illustrates a doctrine seems to call for the addition of a clear ending, in which the prodigal's later conduct is specified.

This passage from Cobbe testifies to the synoptic parables' place in Victorian culture, a place of both immediate familiarity and alienating potential. The parables were part of the received cultural lexicon of that period and were salient landmarks of the religious landscape. They were and are persistently challenging texts, demanding interpretation yet resisting hermeneutical closure. James Stirling wrote in 1873 that Jesus's parables are "not narrower but broader than the Gospels in which they are embedded" (1). That combination of familiarity and flexibility, of iconicity and iconoclasm, made them useful for innovative and subversive purposes in the hands of Victorian writers. But the subversiveness enabled by reinscription is not antithetical to the genre, but rather is built into the genre from the beginning. For Jesus's parables themselves drew on the Hebrew scriptural tradition to attack (among other things) the prevailing religious and ethical norms of his day.

Now that literary studies is in the midst of a simultaneous "religious turn" and "ethical turn," the time is right for a renewal of interest in parables, the genre that, more than any other, sits squarely at the intersection of religion, ethics and literature. *Victorian Parables* examines a cluster of novels from the middle decades of the nineteenth century, which incorporate into their formal and thematic fabric an intentional and sustained conversation with one or more parables of Jesus. In novels by Charlotte Yonge, Margaret Oliphant and Charles Dickens, we discover sophisticated modes of appropriation, reinscription, reinterpretation and reformation of the parable texts. These novels were chosen because they not only allude meaningfully to the parables, as many works from that period do, but because in doing so they more or less fully enter the parable tradition by adopting parabolic narrative strategies to establish a particular – and particularly potent – ethical relationship with the reader. The complex dialogues of the fiction with the parables constitute an active and strenuous Victorian engagement with its biblical heritage, its ethical commitments and its aesthetic experiments and achievements.

# Towards a Definition of Parable

Prior to our investigation of the importance of the parables as not only allusive background but also formative matter of some Victorian fiction, it is necessary to present an overview of two related yet distinct subfields: parable studies and parable-in-literature studies.[3] The Greek word *parabole* signifies "throwing alongside" and came to refer to the comparison of one thing to another by proximity and contrast. A parabolic narrative, then, is a narrative laid alongside another narrative for purposes of illumination or challenge. As Mark Turner has shown, parables both tap into and exemplify the hard-wired human tendency to organize experience in the form of story.[4] But the genre is older than the Greek term borrowed to describe it. Parables in the Western tradition are principally associated not with their Greek roots but with their Judaic roots, largely as mediated to the West through Christianity.[5] In Hebrew, the word *mashal* (from the root *mšl*, meaning "to be like" and translated *parabole* in the Septuagint) carried a very wide range of signification, including figurative devices we know under the names of metaphor, proverb, analogy, and trope as well as parable.[6] Such an expansive definition would seem to undermine the usefulness of the term, but in fact it clarifies essential similarities of technique that underlie otherwise divergent literary and rhetorical effects. The story of the Exodus is called a *mashal* in Psalm 78, in that that story carries an analogic and didactic purpose: as God led the early Hebrews to freedom and victory when they trusted in him, so God will again do for the Jewish community that nourishes itself on that story and trusts in God accordingly. Proverbs, too, often encode an analogy or comparison: "He that hath no rule over his own spirit is like a city that is broken down, and without walls" (Prov. 25:28). Jeremy Schipper suggests that *mashal* is not a category of form but of function: it is not defined by a list of textual features but by its use to draw pointed comparisons in concrete situations of conflict.

Just as no image of a created being can represent God (as witness the First Commandment), so no name can denote God, from which principle derives the use of the unpronounceable tetragammon to refer to God. Since, then, all language about God is necessarily figurative, the trope or *mashal* becomes an essential aspect of religious language in Judaism. *Meshalim* are not merely illustrative, ornamental, or mnemonic rhetorical devices, though they certainly can be all these things. They are the essential condition for the people of God to describe, narrate, and relate to God and God's works.

In saying that *meshalim* are ordered to enable God's people not only to describe God but also to relate to God and God's work in the world, I am emphasizing the ineluctable ethical content of parables in the Judeo-Christian tradition. What is "cast alongside" the parable is the life-story – the experiences and especially the choices – of the audience. The paradigmatic instance of this in the Hebrew Scriptures is the prophet Nathan's confrontation of King David over his adultery with Bathsheba and subsequent murder of her husband Uriah.[7] Nathan goes to David with a story:

> There were two men in one city; the one rich, and the other poor. The rich man had exceeding many flocks and herds: But the poor man had nothing, save one little ewe lamb, which he had bought and nourished up: and it grew up together with him, and with

his children; it did eat of his own meat, and drank of his own cup, and lay in his bosom, and was unto him as a daughter. And there came a traveler unto the rich man, and he spared to take of his own flock and of his own herd, to dress for the wayfaring man that was come unto him; but took the poor man's lamb, and dressed it for the man that was come to him. And David's anger was greatly kindled against the man; and he said to Nathan, 'As the Lord liveth, the man that hath done this thing shall surely die: And he shall restore the lamb fourfold, because he did this thing, and because he had no pity.' And Nathan said to David, 'Thou art the man.' (2 Sam. 12:1-7)

Several important features of parable come into focus in this example. The parable is an indictment of sin, a condemnation of a man's grave transgressions against justice. The parable is directed against the powerful, to one perhaps inclined to see himself as master of the Law rather than as accountable to it. The parable works on David as it does because the analogical approach to the judgment against David disarms his self-protective justifications, eliciting from the king himself a condemnation that would not be permitted against the king in the mouth of another. This analogy between the story and the life of the hearer is brought home in an unexpected reversal that brings self-recognition, not unlike Aristotle's notion of *peripeteia*.[8] Finally, though David gets some obvious interpretative help from Nathan, the complete interpretation of the parable occurs in David's embodied response, a response which takes the form of acts and words of penitence: wearing sackcloth, putting ashes on his head, fasting, tearing his clothes, and writing Psalm 51.

Other examples from the Hebrew Scriptures, while less dramatic than this one, also use analogical or allegorical narratives to convict the people of God with their sin. Ezekiel, perhaps the chief parabolist of the Hebrew Scriptures, compares Israel to an abandoned baby adopted by a loving caretaker only to reject him, to a cooking pot from which the good parts will be removed and the undesirable parts left behind (a figure of the Babylonian exile), and to a vine (Israel) forcibly transplanted by an eagle (the king of Babylon).[9] Ezekiel's *meshalim* include performative acts as well as stories and analogies: he enacts the siege of Jerusalem by lying on his side in front of a model of the city and eating starvation rations cooked over dung, and he draws attention to the unmourned fall of Jerusalem by not mourning the death of his wife. All of these acts are done to arrest the attention of Ezekiel's fellow exiles and lead them to ask in their perplexity, "Wilt thou not tell us what these things are to us, that thou doest so?" (Ez. 24:19). While Nathan's parable to David elicited (self-) condemnation of the sinner, Ezekiel's parables elicit awareness of the people's dire moral and physical state so as to confront them with a choice: "Repent, and turn yourselves from all your transgressions; so iniquity shall not be your ruin" (Ez. 18:30).

Jesus's parables in the gospels clearly arise out of this tradition.[10] Some of the briefer ones are much like proverbs: "The kingdom of heaven is like unto leaven, which a woman took, and hid in three measures of meal, till the whole was leavened" (Matt. 13:33).[11] Many of the longer, narrative ones, including most of the best-known parables, are framed as indictments of the over-confident religiosity of the Pharisees and scribes. Though not politically powerful in first-century Palestine, the Pharisees did enjoy a position of social and cultural privilege by virtue of their guardianship of the Law. As interpreters and, when possible, enforcers of the Mosaic Law in the Jewish community, the Pharisees as described in the gospels substituted on some level control of the Law and its application for their own accountability to it. The parable of the prodigal son targets the Pharisees who, like the older brother, preen themselves on their exemplary external conduct while uncharitably scorning and excluding those whose sin is more visible. The parable of the Good Samaritan indicts the religious elite for allowing ritual observance to displace loving one's neighbor. The parable of the wicked tenants directly condemns the self-serving misappropriation of power by the same religious elite. The parable of the Pharisee and the publican declares that the self-confessed sinner went home justified before God because of his repentance, while the self-professed Law-keeper went home alienated from God because of his self-righteousness.[12] In each of these instances, the parable's import is borne in through a reversal in which the expected moral approbation is reversed: the wastrel son is celebrated, the flagrant sinner is justified, and the hated half-breed behaves more like a child of God than the ritually and racially pure sons of Abraham. In other parables, God is figured in a seemingly irreverent light as an unjust judge, a tyrannical king, or an uncaring neighbor. The striking images and reversals not only "tease [the mind] into active thought" to make sense of the seeming incongruities (Dodd 16), but they also demand an embodied response to the challenge they pose. The invitation to think very differently about something one thought one knew carries with it an invitation to act very differently, according to a new construal of reality.

# Interpreting the Parables: A Brief History

The parables of Jesus in the synoptic gospels upset the religious applecart, rearrange fixed categories of social and moral hierarchy, and provoke puzzlement and sometimes fury. What is to be done with these stories that are homey yet alienating, foundational to Christianity yet persistently iconoclastic?

From late antiquity to the late nineteenth century, the prevailing mode of interpreting the parables was by means of allegory. The parable, like all the Scripture, had to be read in its "spiritual sense" for its right meaning to be understood. In Augustine's famous exegesis of the parable of the Good Samaritan, for example, the traveler is a figure for Adam who in turn is a figure for all humanity. The journey from Jerusalem to Jericho represents humanity's descent from the celestial city of God to fallen, mortal life. The thieves are devils, the wounds are sins, the Levite and priest represent the Old Testament, and the Samaritan is a figure for Christ. The oil and wine refer to hope and the exhortation to good works (or to baptism in other readings). The inn is the Church, with the Apostle Paul as the innkeeper. The two coins used to pay the innkeeper are the commands to love God and neighbor, or in other readings, the promise of life in this life and that to come.[13] The Christian humanists and the Reformers rejected some of the particular readings and applications, usually substituting others, but they largely left the practice of allegoresis intact.[14]

Adolf Jülicher inaugurated the modern critical study of the synoptic parables in his two-volume work *Die Gleichnisreden Jesu* (1888 and 1899). Jülicher insisted that allegorical interpretation was a wrong-headed imposition of classical methods on biblical texts. The authentic meaning of Jesus's parables would have been transparent in their original context – Jesus did not expect his simple-minded hearers to undertake ingenious hermeneutical gymnastics like Augustine's. Jülicher argued that when its original content and context is recovered, each parable delivers a single and generalizable teaching, usually about moral conduct.

C. H. Dodd's groundbreaking work on the parables in 1936 brought Jülicher's conclusions to the English-speaking world and adduced some important developments to them. Like Jülicher, Dodd argued that each parable illustrates a single truth that is best grasped through a picture or brief story. But parables are not merely elaborate conveyances for moral commonplaces, as Jülicher had indicated, but rather the urgent expression of the new reality of the kingdom of God which Jesus proclaimed. The true meaning of the parables can only be learned by peeling off accreted layers of interpretation imposed by the early church to recover the *Sitz im Leben* ("setting in life," the world of thought and experience) of their original telling. At the center of that *Sitz im Leben* is Jesus's heralding of the kingdom of God, so Dodd comes to read the parables as so many expressions of Jesus's claims for a realized eschatology.[15] Joachim Jeremias embraced Dodd's *Sitz im Leben* approach in his influential 1947 work *The Parables of Jesus*, though he expanded the purview of the parables beyond the kingdom of God to encompass a number of other concerns.

The Dodd-Jeremias approach, as it came to be called, set the terms of parable study for at least a generation. Its strenuous efforts at historical reconstruction are no doubt indispensible: one must try to understand, for example, the complex social, racial, and political connotations of the label "Samaritan" in first-century Palestine in order to form even a rudimentary sense of what the parable of the Good Samaritan is saying. However, its weaknesses gradually became apparent. In particular, critics addressed how the *Sitz-im-Leben* approach mistakenly limited the parable's meaning to its original intention and reception, denying both the possibility of its continued relevance and the importance of its aesthetic form. Other critics focused on the futility of fixing that original intention and reception in the first place, preferring instead to look at the parables' literary relatedness to the stories in which they are set. Both responses were influenced by developments in literary studies.

The interrelation of parable exegesis and literary studies was influenced and encouraged by the movement known as narrative theology. Though thinking about theology in terms of narrative has always necessarily been a feature of Christianity and Judaism, the role of narrative in theological thought was suppressed for much of the modern period, as Hans Frei showed in his groundbreaking book *The Eclipse of Biblical Narrative* (1974). Frei identified the intellectual developments and theoretical missteps of the eighteenth and nineteenth centuries that resulted in the conceptual separation of the stories told in the Bible from their putative meaning. Once the meaning is extracted, the story is set aside, relegated to the role of illustration or aid to memory. One result is that the indeterminacy intrinsic to narrative is suppressed in favor of the propositional claims that are presumed to constitute the text's "real" or meaningful content.[16] Narrative theology, then, emphasizes that people can only know God through the story of God's relations with people, and that the people of God can only be so by participating in that story, or by identifying their life story with the story of God's work to redeem the world.[17] Such an understanding privileges the literary form of the scripture text and demands that the study of theology tap into the tools of literary analysis on some level.

To understand Christianity foundationally as an ordering of life under the rubric of participation in a transnational, transgenerational story helps to make room for the parables in Christian thinking. If Christianity is a set of doctrines that must be rightly believed, or a set of precepts that must be rightly followed, then polysemeity is a threat rather than an opportunity. Under the model of religion as doctrinal and ethical conformity, the burden of theology is to close all the wrong doors of interpretation so that only the right ones are left open. Texts such as parables that seem to open more doors than they close then have to be contained, delimited, and shown to correspond with existing propositions. Theology understood as narrative, however, can embrace complexly interwoven stories and stories within stories, exploring polysemeity as an opportunity rather than a problem.[18]

In his study of parables, Dan O. Via drew on the emerging ideas of narrative theology to chart a way forward from the dead-end of *Sitz im Leben* yet without a simple return to allegorizing.[19] He rejected the "severely historical" *Sitz im Leben* approach for limiting the parable's legitimate meaning to the one point which was intended and understood by the original audience (though he does not lodge the more postmodern critique that that original understanding is permanently unavailable).[20] At the same time Via's recovery of the importance of the formal, literary qualities of the parables never resorted to allegoresis in which each element in a parable is said to signify directly a particular element in another system or story. Rather, he called for readings that explore the "total configuration" of story elements and crucially the "understanding of existence implied in the plots – in the human encounters and their outcomes" (93, 95). Though he has been fairly criticized for neglecting the parables' historical context altogether, Via's major contribution, in my view, was to insist on the parables being both aesthetic productions (against biblical scholars of his day who viewed the parables as material from which a "point" must be extracted) and as having an existential-theological dimension (against the New Critics of his day who held that any literary work was entirely self-contained). Right reading of the parables, Via suggested, requires keeping alive the tension between their literary and theological dimensions. Definitions of either "theology" or "literature" that exclude the possibility of this tension need to be reconsidered in light of the parable (70–71).

The direction one goes with the literary approach to the parables depends significantly on what literary theory one subscribes to. One school of thought adopted an essentially New Critical approach to the parables, dropping the Dodd-Jeremias concern with source-criticism to privilege instead questions about the role played by a parable or group of parables in a given gospel text.[21] Another influential approach was the "New Hermeneutic" line, whose foremost Anglo-American proponent is Robert Funk. The New Hermeneutics emphasized that parables are "language-events" in which the reader's response is revelatory or formational to and of the reader.[22] Parables do not merely describe the kingdom of God, but rather as speech acts they *create* for the audience an experience of the radical otherness of the kingdom of God in the ministry of Jesus. This experience of radical otherness is felt in the paradoxical combination or juxtaposition of everydayness and strangeness that parables contain. The familiarity of the parable's settings and situations builds a connection to the reader's experience, but the startling reversal of the parable's climax challenges the presumed normativity of that experience with a radically new normativity brought by Jesus, which the reader is invited to share (Funk, *Language* 158–162). Parables are not reducible to either platitude or proposition because this existential potency lies irreducibly in the narrative itself. Parables can therefore be said to interpret the reader, in that the reader's response of joyful acceptance or suspicious rejection of the parable reveals whether or not he participates in the kingdom of God (Funk, *Language* 11–12, 16–17).²³ In emphasizing this revelatory and performative character, however, Funk shortchanges the fact that *what* the parables reveal entails a distinctive ontology and an ethics.

Other readings of the parables influenced by literary studies include structuralist, poststructuralist, feminist, Foucauldian, and Freudian approaches.²⁴ In many of these cases it has not been easy for theorists to maintain both sides of Via's tension between the theological and literary dimensions of this genre. Taking the cue from Via, Funk, and others that parables are not to be understood as having a single historically fixed meaning, exegetes have increasingly developed interpretations that not only separate the parables from their place in Christianity, but also sometimes deny there being any theological or ethical content to the parables at all. A salient instance of the latter is the work of John Dominic Crossan, whose later work moved from structuralist into poststructuralist readings of Jesus's parables as sheer linguistic play. The only content or meaning that Crossan allows to be signalled by the parables is the fictionality and self-referentiality of language. "Parable is paradox made into story," he announces, and "Paradox is language laughing at itself" (*Raid* 93). The result of that syllogism, of course, is that parable is story-language laughing at language. In Crossan's interpretation, the parable of the sower is a "metaparable of hermeneutical polyvalence" – a darkly comic story about the proliferation of spurious meanings from gnomic sayings (*Cliffs* 54). Its message is that there is no message, so interpreters should "give it up" and enjoy the joke (*Cliffs* 55). Crossan's view of parable implicitly denies the existence of parable within Christianity per se.²⁵ To subscribe to the hegemonic metanarrative of Christianity, as he sees it, is necessarily to reject the counter-hegemonic message of parable, the mini-narrative that is by definition nothing more or less than the gadfly of all metanarratives.

To summarize, it seems that we may trace the modern history of parable studies in terms of its emphases and omissions. Jülicher emphasized their simplicity and didacticism and ignored their literary character. Dodd saw their function in revealing a present eschatology and therefore their historical realism but neglected the parables' relevance outside of their original context. Via restored interest in the parables as literary texts at the expense of ignoring their place in history. Funk explored their revelatory effect through their narrativity but downplayed their didacticism. Crossan revelled in their paradox and polyvalence but rejected the possibility of their affirmative content. Each figure brought to light neglected aspects of parable studies, but few managed to keep the complicated whole in view.[26]

Parables are the complex, puzzling, system-defying texts that they are because of how they work on several axes at once: they are literary and theological, subversive and constructive, historical and timeless, iconic and iconoclastic. The challenge to the interpreter is not to allow some of these aspects to close down others, even or perhaps especially when they are contradictory. We must make room for the parables' unsettling, subversive effect *and* for their foundational place in the Christian story. To remove parables from their tensive place in Christianity and to place them in a pristine and inaccessible realm of "pure" subversiveness, as Crossan does, is just another mode of cancelling out their complexity and flattening them into one dimension. To read parables well we have to be more open to polyvalence even than Crossan: open enough to consider the possibility that the parables say something affirmative of theological import, while always resisting the tendency to reduce them to moral precepts or theological propositions.

## Interpreting the Parables: Paul Ricoeur's Theory

The most comprehensive and instructive theoretical understanding of the parables emerges from Paul Ricoeur's work in response to Via, Crossan, and others.[27] Ricoeur describes a parable as a metaphor transposed into story. Metaphor combines two things that do not belong together to forge a novel reality: a new idea in which one or both things are conceptually transformed by being seen in the light of the other (79–80). A metaphor lives only while it is conceptually innovative: once a metaphor has been assimilated into conventional thought it is said to be "dead." Parable achieves this creation of a new reality in the mode of narrative, which is to say in the mode of plot. Readings of the parables which emphasize their metaphoricity often give short shrift to their essential narrativity. The two dissimilar things that are joined to create the novel reality are the everyday and the extravagant, hyperbolic or paradoxical (125). The *frisson* that makes a parable lies in the juxtaposition of an ordinary situation, plot and set of characters with an extraordinary, unpredictable turn of action, which forces a total reconception of the whole situation in the light of the new reality imaged in that turn. A parable is therefore "a fiction capable of redescribing life" in startlingly unfamiliar terms by means of an extravagant reversal (89). The audience's response to the parable occurs in the gap between the expected and the unexpected, the familiar and the alien. The effect of that gap on the reader can range from puzzling to disorienting to confrontational to infuriating, depending on how deeply invested one is in the everyday conceptual scheme posited in the parable's realist basis. Like metaphors, parables can be dead if the high relief between the everyday and the extravagant becomes eroded by familiarity; however, parables can maintain their living power more successfully than can simple metaphors because of the hermeneutical richness of story (31).

A son's rebellion, a traveller attacked, a landowner hiring workers all through the day – these are realistic situations that operate according to what Bernard Harrison calls "the everyday morality which we all know well enough how to handle" (234). The prodigal son knows not to expect a son's welcome from the father he has scorned and plans to beg only to be received as a hired servant; workers hired late in the day expect to receive a smaller wage. Extravagance or unexpected reversals occur in the father's joyous welcome, in the despised Samaritan's offering aid when the members of the religious establishment refused it, and the landowner's decision to pay a full day's wage to those who worked only one hour as well as those who worked all day long. The parables stage what Charles Hedrick calls a "clash of fictions" and what Harrison more aptly calls a dramatic contrast between rival "conceptual scheme[s] in terms of which [their] hearers construe the world and their lives in it" (Hedrick, *Parables* 73, Harrison 226).[28]

Much of this account sounds like Funk's understanding of the parables as language-events, but Ricoeur's theory proves to be more supple in its ability to comprehend ethical and political as well as theological and literary dimensions of the parables. Ricoeur's theory accommodates differences of opinion about the specific nature of the familiar and the alien conceptual schemes being juxtaposed. In the parable of the workers in the vineyard, traditional exegesis sees a contrast between a Law-oriented Judaism and the new Christian order of grace given to latecomers. A reformed exegesis might see a contrast between salvation earned by works and salvation by faith alone. Harrison sees a contrast between an economic system ordered to the owner's profit and an economic system ordered to the provision of a living wage to all members of the community. For Crossan the parable stages a contrast between the expected and the surprising per se, in a studious avoidance of what he calls "irrelevant moral considerations" (*Raid* 161–62, *In Parables* 114). Irrespective of whether the parable is principally understood as referring to soteriology, to economic justice or to linguisticality, the parable's power lies in the replacing of one conceptual scheme with another.

Where the lines fall in delimiting these "old" and "new" conceptual schemes will depend on where one stands historically and ideologically. For much of Christian history, it was axiomatic to equate the "old" with Judaism and the "new" with Christianity.[29] But these categories of old and new continued to shift throughout the history of the interpretation and appropriation of the parables. The rapid production of diverse readings of the parables in the last half-century reveals, if nothing else, that today's revolution is tomorrow's cliché. Hence the eagerness of scholars to push past the ever-mounting clichés and express the newest "new" that can be found in the parables. This drive is understandable: if the parables' enduring power lies in their ability to overturn normative conceptual schemes, then reading the parables requires a continual openness to the new unseating the old.

However, as we have seen, this process can fail in another way, by refusing to see the possibility of affirmative or disclosive content in the parables. Ricoeur's theory escapes that problem by returning to the question of what is the referent of the parables – what is the nature of the new reality they shadow forth or (as the New Hermeneutics would have it) bring about? He answers that the referent of the parables is the kingdom of God, which he understands to be symbolic shorthand for a transformed, perfected human existence: "human reality in its wholeness" (127). This transformed human existence is a matter of politics no less than personal morality, a matter of economics no less than soteriology, and a matter of ecology no less than eschatology, because God's salvation of human beings is constituted in terms of the redemption of all of creation (126–27). Ricoeur rejects the possibility that parables express "paradox lived out in loneliness and impotence" – an apparent reference to the sterility of Crossan's readings of the parables as entirely self-referential.[30] Rather, a parable "disorients only to reorient" the audience along the lines of perfected, redeemed human life (126).

This sense of the referent of the parables allows for polyvalent interpretation while still reining in excesses of deconstruction like Crossan's reading. It accommodates applications related to economics and politics, but keeps those applications moored in a theological context: "Paradox then does not strike *praxis* any less than it does *theoria*, political *praxis* any less than the *praxis* of private morality. It just prevents us from converting religious discourse entirely into political discourse – for the same reasons that it forbids its conversion into moral discourse" (Ricoeur 127). Also, this understanding of the parables' referent means that they can never be contained within a fixed framework. Because they point to nothing less than perfection (what Ricoeur calls "limit-experience"), they will always be disruptive to any humanly conceivable theological or political program. This view allows us to hold in tension the parables' iconoclasm with their iconicity, their polyvalence with their referentiality, and their performativity with their didacticism.

## Theorizing Extrabiblical Parables

Extending this understanding of the synoptic parables into our consideration of extrabiblical parables (an extension Ricoeur himself does not offer to make) yields a view of parables in literature that is both more comprehensive and more precise than much of the work that has been done on parables in literature. Ricoeur's emphasis on the parables' narrativity – on the tension that is made out of the reversals of plot – allows us to define extrabiblical parables in terms of a narrative strategy rather than in terms of accidental formal qualities (such as length) or ideological qualities (such as Christian – or anti-Christian – teaching). The narrative strategy that characterizes parable is the staging of a gap between everyday human experience and a gesture of extravagance that points to human limit-experience. This strategy is performative: it involves the reader in a process of discerning and reacting to the gap. It is also perlocutionary: it is completed only in the embodied response of the reader. Its vision of limit-experience is confrontational and disorienting, particularly in that it exposes the reader's complicity with the everyday conceptual scheme that the parable puts under critical scrutiny. None of this is necessarily Christian, of course, but because of the place of the parables in Christianity, it should be possible to find instances of it in the writing of Christians. We should be prepared to see that the literary reinscription of parables constitutes an important element in the church's ongoing hermeneutical engagement with the parables of Jesus.

In addition to this greater precision and comprehensiveness, Ricoeur's theory suggests the importance of historicizing extrabiblical parables against the conventions of their day. If the narrative strategy of parable is to stage the gap between the "old" religious or moral convention and the "new" refreshed conceptual scheme that points towards limit-experience, then it is necessary to consider any particular extrabiblical parable against the prevailing homiletic and theological readings of its time (as well as against the literary conventions of its time) for its parabolic qualities to be realized. Seeing such works as disruptive to convention requires us to be sufficiently attuned to the conventions of their specific historical moments. Otherwise we will only find parables among the relatively recent texts that confront conventions we recognize as those of our own time or of recent memory.

A survey of studies of extrabiblical parables reveals that this limitation has in fact been widespread: such studies invariably privilege modernist and experimental fiction. There are good and obvious reasons for this. Modernist writers such as Kafka and Borges made a self-conscious return to the genre in their various literary challenges to the ideological and literary commonplaces of their times. If parables entail subversion of norms, then we will naturally look for them among the most spectacularly innovative narratives. But we must also recognize that in other historical periods, the gap between the conventional conceptual scheme and the innovative conceptual scheme was located differently, and parables of those times may be expected to offer equally disruptive dissonances in ways that speak to their moment.

In the 1970s and 1980s, a rush of studies on parables in literature followed the flood of parable studies by religious scholars in the 1960s and 1970s.[31] This material is marked by some of the same understandable but problematic tendencies that we have seen in parable studies directly. Informed by his Derridean view of parables as self-referential linguistic play, Crossan finds in Jorge Luis Borges the truest successor to Jesus as parabolist (*Raid on the Articulate*). Funk similarly sees Kafka as a parabolist who disrupts the old verities of his time with a new, modernist sensibility (*Jesus as Precursor*). But this eagerness to identify parables with subversiveness per se means that these scholars have eyes only for literary parables that are not only extrabiblical but also antibiblical. Crossan in particular, having identified parables as being on the opposite pole from "myth" (his term for established, world-ordering narratives), can only find bona fide parables among modern experimental writers and only outside Christianity. Funk is right that the burden of an exegete of the parables is to make possible something like the experience of hearing the parable fresh, as its first hearers heard it. Crossan in fact does this in explicating the parable of the Good Samaritan in terms of Ireland's Catholic-Protestant conflict (*Dark Interval* 86–87), or in suggesting that the parable of the Pharisee and the publican be retold with the pope and a pimp ("No matter where the story goes after such an opening the narrator has placed himself in jeopardy by the initial juxtaposition" [*Raid* 108–9]). But these critics miss the fact that this kind of potent retelling is not just the project of twentieth-century anti-religionists, who have boldly shaken off the trappings of sanitized and domesticated Christianity. It is in fact an ongoing project within the church's own history of grappling with the parables, especially by writers, as such salient examples as Søren Kierkegaard, Fyodor Dostoevsky, Flannery O'Connor and Marilynne Robinson make clear.

A similar omission can be seen in the work of Frank Kermode. Kermode's *The Genesis of Secrecy* is a justly acclaimed treatment of the gospels, especially Mark, alongside modern literature and towards a nuanced theory of interpretation. Kermode takes the parable genre as a paradigm for narratives that paradoxically conceal and reveal, including works by James Joyce, Harry Green, Thomas Pynchon, and Franz Kafka. Like those authors, he's not interested in resolving the reveal/conceal paradox but in magnifying its irresolvability. Playing to his dominant trope of the text's construction of the reader or interpreter into the roles of "insider" or "outsider," Kermode claims that the hermeneutical problems raised in and by the gospels need to be unpacked by an outsider to Christianity like himself.[32] Kermode seems to assume that the outsider's freedom from bias will avert premature foreclosure of interpretative possibilities, but the book shows rather that the outsider's particular bias merely forecloses an alternative set of interpretative possibilities, namely, the possibility that the gospel of Mark contains affirmative and disclosive content and not just delightfully perverse riddles.[33]

Kermode suggests that good readings (i.e., readings that are not theologically predetermined) remain eternally open to spiraling deconstructive possibilities. This view is similar to Crossan's take on the parables as nothing more or less than playful metafiction. But this understanding would seem to require us to read the gospels not just as literary constructs, but rather as literary constructs of a particular type, namely, the modernist experimental novel. Reading Mark against Joyce's *Ulysses*, Kermode seems to come close to suggesting that Jesus told parables to keep professors busy for all time, like Joyce claimed, probably tongue-in-cheek, to have done in *Ulysses*. As is the case with Crossan, Kermode's sense of modernist secularism as the "new" that upsets the "old" of fusty religion leads him to align ancient parables with modernist ones. This alignment is legitimate, but it leaves a significant part of the story of extrabiblical parables not only untold, but completely unacknowledged.

Sallie McFague TeSelle, unlike Crossan, Funk and Kermode, is open to finding parabolic narratives in mimetic fiction and in work by Christians. In a winsome recapitulation of the New Hermeneutic view, she suggests that the effect of the parable on the audience is uniquely important to interpretation, "because there is a stress in the parables on confrontation and decision" (*Speaking* 73). But when TeSelle proceeds to examine literature as parable, she strangely loses sight of these nuances. Her discussion of fiction centers on Alan Paton, Flannery O'Connor and J. R. R. Tolkien (after setting aside *The Brothers Karamazov* and *The Sound and the Fury* as "too easy" to discuss as parables!) (*Speaking* 132). What she finds in these novels is indirect depictions of conversion or of the mysterious working of grace in human affairs. She is silent about how the stories strike the reader, or how the authors' narrative choices condition or generate a readerly experience of "shock to the imagination."[34] While I agree that these novels offer the insights she finds, that reading is a long way from the "stress on confrontation and decision" she described as characteristic of parables.

It would seem that an extended study of extrabiblical parabolic literature well grounded in both literary and exegetical theory and practice is yet to be performed. Crossan, Funk and Kermode operate with a one-sided understanding of parables that overdetermines the sort of literary parables they can identify or discuss. TeSelle fails to deploy the fullness of her parable theory in reading literature. Gila Safran Naveh's comparative study of parables aspires to comprehensiveness by including discussions of ancient Hebrew, synoptic, rabbinic, medieval and modern parables as successive snapshots of a developing genre. However, the strength of her project lies in her treatment of the Jewish parable tradition; her study includes no extrabiblical parables in the Christian tradition. Her conclusion that parables artfully reflect the epistemological as well as ideological norms of their time, evolving their message in response to those norms as perceived by the authors, is undeniable but not very illuminating. Nor does it go far enough to show how parables problematize as well as reflect their culture's received opinions. Kevin Mills's creative and idiosyncratic *The Prodigal Sign: A Parable of Criticism* studies the parable of the prodigal son as a parable of literary criticism. His astute readings of Shakespeare, Helen Keller and David Storey (among others) center around the trope of prodigality as a figure for escape and return, which he refracts through his experiences as a literary critic, professional academic and child of a Baptist minister.

On the literary-critical side, the mishandling of parable is usually a matter of theoretical neglect. The word "parable" shows up often enough in literary criticism, but it is rarely examined or even defined.[35] Rather the word is used gesturally to assert that the work has some (usually unspecified) quality of a religious or moral nature. To take a couple of recent examples, Edwin Arnold's reading of Cormac McCarthy's novels as "moral parables" argues for the novels' submerged yet palpable resistance to the nihilism expressed by many of the characters. Steven Shively's reference to Willa Cather's "parables of sacrifice" means only that Cather uses Christian symbolism to convey her themes of sacrifice and redemption. Yet parable is at other times invoked to suggest the opposite: that the work is subversive of religious or moral affirmation. Steven Doloff reads Melville's "Bartleby the Scrivener" as a parody of the parable of the Good Samaritan, and Mike Riggs reads Eugene O'Neill's Dynamo Cycle as a set of "parables against religion." Robert Eisenhauer's *Parables of Disfiguration* falls in this category, though Eisenhauer never addresses what he means by "parable." The two uses of the term – as vaguely religious or irreligious – collide in Janet Larson's study of biblical allusion in Dickens, where she resorts to the phrase "dark parables" to describe Dickens's negative portrayals of the moral failures of his society. Apparently they are parables in that they have moral content, but they are dark parables because they reflect the actual negation of traditional values.

The problem is not that the word "parable," like the parables themselves, is polyvalent, but that its polyvalence is not acknowledged or theorized. In general, literary critics make "parable" into too broad a category: it refers to a vaguely Christian sensibility, possibly in the mode of fable or allegory. Alternatively, as in an essay by J. Hillis Miller, parable is an intensified instance of indirect discourse; thus it loses its distinctiveness by becoming a synecdoche of all literature ("Parable and Performative"). Theologians, on the other hand, typically make "parable" into too narrow a category, reserving it for its obvious instantiations in short stories that induce a sort of ideological vertigo.

I have already described how Ricoeur's notion of parable will enable a consideration of extrabiblical parables in terms of narrative strategy; this approach both broadens and narrows the field. It narrows the field by focusing on texts that perform something like the narrative strategy I have described, thus excluding parable lookalikes such as fables and exemplary or illustrative tales. However, it more substantially broadens the field by suggesting that parables can be found among novels and other extended narratives.

This study will focus on a few instances of parabolic fiction in mid-nineteenth-century Britain, a choice which offers several advantages. First, it makes possible a degree of historicizing that most parable-in-literature studies forfeit, whether by necessity or by choice. Reading these novels against the backdrop of relevant contemporaneous theological, ecclesiological, ethical, and aesthetic norms and conflicts will help bring into sharper focus how the parabolic strategies of these novels operate in challenging contemporaneous norms. Second, the choice of Victorian Britain is particularly illuminating for this sort of historicized reading of extrabiblical parables given that the Bible retained a strong cultural and religious currency and even authority in Victorian Britain, yet its uses and meanings were vigorously contested. Recent research has demonstrated that the nineteenth century saw multiple and developing dynamic clashes over religion, not the gradual suffocation of socially irrelevant belief that was pictured by an earlier generation of historians. It is not only that Victorian engagements with parables illuminate these live tensions. Rather, the role of parables both within and against the Christian tradition makes the literary reinscription of parables a particularly apt occasion for the period's contests over Christianity and the Bible. Third, given the preoccupations of Victorian realism, the challenges for narration and interpretation posed by parables are particularly well-suited to aspects of the realist project. Recent work on realism and ethics makes clear that the dominant literary modes of the nineteenth century were characterized by a heightened ethical consciousness. However, this important dimension of the fiction remains relatively unexplored, and the obvious relationship between Christianity and narrative ethics during this time has been almost ignored. As a biblical form with an ethical bearing, the parable genre uniquely enables the overlapping discussion of religious and ethical concerns in literature.

Taken together, these facts indicate that Victorian Britain offers an immensely fertile occasion for studying the rich and contested intersections of religion, ethics, and literary art. I offer, then, not a diachronic overview of the continuities and discontinuities observable in the genre of parable, but rather a synchronic examination of parabolic narrative strategy in a time when Christian cultural capital was both pervasive and contested. In the process, I argue against the widespread critical assumption that interesting or worthy parables in literature are only to be found in non-mimetic texts and texts outside the Christian tradition. My second chapter will develop and defend these claims.

# 2

# The Extraordinary in the Ordinary: Parable and Realism

My approach to reading parables narratologically reveals unexpected correspondences between first-century parables and nineteenth-century realism. Nevertheless, choosing Victorian fiction as the locus of this study of parables in literature immediately involves me in a number of problems and critical controversies. One set of objections is posed by some prominent parable-in-literature scholars whose work I surveyed in the previous chapter. In the story they tell, parables and realism are necessarily antithetical to each other. In its strongest form, this position categorically denies the possibility that a realist narrative, let alone a long, multiplot realist novel, can be parabolic; in its less strident forms, it may remain agnostic on the question of realism's compatibility with parable or may even theoretically admit such compatibility, but in actual fact, avoids any discussion of realist texts. For most of these scholars, the realist novel is one-dimensional, and that dimension is ideologically conservative and epistemologically reassuring, while parables, of course, are the opposite. A different set of difficulties appears in the work of many Victorianists, who have found that formal realism is ideologically complicated, epistemologically challenging and linguistically sophisticated. But these recognitions are often accompanied by a set of default assumptions about the flatness and increasing irrelevancy of religious belief in the period. These assumptions often lead to the stated or unstated conclusion that realism is interesting and complicated in the ways just described because of its resistance to religion. Its resistance may be intentional or unintentional, but it is in any case relatively successful, and the enduring interest of the genre depends on its escape from religious paradigms.

In this chapter, I address both sets of problems, arguing, in the first instance, that much important recent work on realism decisively demonstrates the parabolic potential of the Victorian realist novel. This first stage of the argument will begin with a brief consideration of the presence of realism in the parables of Jesus, before moving forward to draw on recent work by Victorianists that suggests the potential for overlap between realism and parable. This research not only refutes the flat caricature of the realist novel, but it also develops a theory of realism that is quite compatible with the notion of parable that I outlined in the first chapter. In the second instance, I show that this nuanced conception of realism has not yet been extended into consideration of the religious dimensions of realist novels. In some cases, any possible religious dimensions have been denied with some vehemence. Finally, I point towards the gains to be found by reading some Victorian novels through the lens of the parable genre and of the actual parables of Jesus.

## The Mimetic Character of Parables

When asked to respond directly to Paul Ricoeur's theory of parable, John Dominic Crossan identified his essential disagreement with Ricoeur's thought as follows: whereas Ricoeur held that parables consist of "the extraordinary in the ordinary," Crossan held that parables are altogether on the side of the extraordinary (*Cliffs* 19). Parables for Ricoeur are defined by their extravagant plot reversals that destabilize the realism of the narrative, arresting readers' attention to an expression of limit-experience, or perfected human existence. Parables for Crossan, on the other hand, have no stake in the imitative portrayal of the real world; on the contrary, they are preoccupied with exposing the self-referential linguisticality of all existence. We have seen in Chapter 1 the assumptions that lie upstream from this view and some of the implications that lie downstream from it. What we have to consider now is another of those implications: the rejection of the possibility that realism can have any place in parable.

Not only do Crossan and Kermode prefer to find extrabiblical parables in modernist experimental fiction, but they also reject the possibility of realist fiction being parabolic. For Crossan, this rejection is explicit and scornful. In *Raid on the Articulate*, the realist novel, "that beloved child born to Mimesis in the years of its dotage," is the foil to Borges's bold and playful parabolic writing (77). Crossan assumes that realist fiction is captive to what he calls the Mimetic Fallacy: "to say that reality-out-there is copied with mimetic fidelity in any book" (*Raid* 89). In a similar vein, he insists that parables must be very short indeed: any significant length in a narrative becomes an attempt to order reality, whereas parables always and only work to dissolve the apparent solidity of our linguistic existence (*Cliffs* 3).[1]

Kermode, for his part, acknowledges that parabolic narratives can be found in narratives that appear transparent, and he suggests that parables can be found in long as well as in short texts (*Genesis* 34–41). However, his own glancing overview of hermeneutically interesting narratives contains nothing that falls chronologically between Laurence Sterne and James Joyce. In exploring the parabolic qualities of experimental fiction, he remarks, "Not for nothing ... does [the *nouveau roman*] wage its campaign against vulgar mimesis" (*Genesis* 117). A similar omission can be seen in J. Hillis Miller's "Parable and Performative in the Gospels and in Modern Literature." Miller implies that the category of parable extends more or less to all indirect discourse of a narrative sort, but he discusses parables in connection with twentieth-century literature only, in spite of being a senior statesman of Victorian literary studies.

The view of parables and realism as mutually exclusive entails errors about parable no less than about realism. The response to the former error is already implicit in what we have been saying about parable. Ricoeur's understanding of parable as capturing *"the extraordinary in the ordinary"* reminds us that a parable, to be decipherable and therefore effective, must have some grounds of overlap with the reader's lived experience (Ricoeur 115, emphasis in original). Without the ordinary or everyday basis for the story, the unexpected or extravagant reversal would have no traction in the reader's mind: "this realism ... precisely heightens the eccentricity of the modes of behavior to which the Kingdom of Heaven is compared" (115).[2] Amos Wilder similarly emphasizes that the everydayness of the parables is a necessary condition for the kind of existential confrontation that the parables pose to their readers: "The parables make men give attention, come alive, and face things. And they do this by evoking men's everyday experience" (*Early Christian Rhetoric* 75). By this token, though Wilder does not draw the point, the wholly disorienting, vertiginous parables of the modernists may be less well-suited to the confrontational and revelatory function of parables than Crossan and Funk have supposed. Similarly, David Parris has recently argued for mimesis as the foundational condition for the parables to operate. If some basis in the everyday is a prerequisite for the parable's reversal to strike with a disorienting effect, then we might expect to find more potential for parable in mimetic modes of storytelling than has been supposed.

## The Parabolic Character of Realism

The latter error, that of equating realism with a naïvely transparent view of reality, has been much discussed in Victorian studies. There is a well-established history of challenges to the reductive picture of realism as self-assured of its transparent referentiality. George Levine's *The Realistic Imagination* is one of the early high points of this history; it influentially demonstrated that realism is "not a solidly self-satisfied vision based in a misguided objectivity and faith in representation, but a highly self-conscious attempt to explore or create a new reality" (*Realistic Imagination* 19–20).[3] I will press this issue further with the help of Harry Shaw's recent magisterial *Narrating Reality*, which addresses two key misunderstandings of realism: that it presents a totalistic view of reality and that it purports to give a transparent view of the "real" world outside of language. Both of these sins against postmodern theory conduce to make the genre either banal or politically insidious, or both.

As regards referentiality, Shaw registers some of the consequences of the rapid acceptance of Ian Watt's stark juxtaposition between language that offers itself as a naïve representation of reality and language that is entirely self-referential and therefore avoids bad-faith claims to represent reality. We have already seen how Crossan and Kermode appear captive to this binary. For Shaw, this reductive binary does not do justice to the nuances of realism, which productively mediates between the reader's mind and history because it "supposes that, in our encounters with reality, we can produce new and more adequate knowledge" (33). That knowledge may be put to a variety of political uses. Shaw argues,

> [R]ealism doesn't trade in 'transparent' representation, because it doesn't need to and doesn't want to. Realism doesn't need to, because nothing about the nature of language requires that an attempt to make contact with the real world must involve 'transparent reference' to a putative 'world prior to language.' Realism doesn't want to, because it's often interested in the issue of how we can best come to grips with the world, and because it's always interested in engaging the reader, not in some sort of illusion of 'direct' contact with the world, but in a dialogue in which the stakes are more rhetorical than epistemological and have more to do with the will than with a certain (inadequate) model of knowing. (39)

Though I suspect that the epistemological and the volitional are not as hermeneutically distinct as Shaw here implies, he rightly emphasizes that the realist novel mimics not reality, but how we experience reality: what we know, think we know, and don't and can't know. Rather than seeing fictional referentiality as a matter of "sticking labels on things," Shaw sees fiction as referring to dynamic relationships and structures in a way that is both "in" and "above" the relationships and structures it describes (94, 256). This turn to the larger unit of meaning-carrying discourse to explain how referentiality can occur is similar to Ricoeur's key claim that the unit of reference in discourse is not the word, but rather the sentence (Ricoeur 81 and Shaw 71).

On the issue of realism's totalizing and therefore coercive tendencies, Shaw points out that just as realism has been both praised and denigrated for presenting a totalizing and comprehensive view of reality, so it has more recently been both praised and denigrated for *not* presenting any such totalizing view of reality. The confusion of analysis results from the fact that, by virtue of its chief project, "the claim to place us in history" (36), realism moves between two poles: "faced with a world of diverse historicist particularity, realism attempts to give that world some degree of order while remaining true to its concrete specificity" (32). This "realist problematic" between the ordered whole and the mutinous particularities is distorted when critics focus on only one of the two poles (37).

Moreover, Shaw finds that most readings of realism, whether positive or negative, blithely assume an obtuse reader who is carried along on a stream of self-evident representation that denies the reader interpretative freedom. This assumption matches what we see, for example, in Kermode's urbane shrug at readers' dull and timid "habituat[ion] to the myth of transparency" (*Genesis*118). The view of realism that Shaw expounds, in which the novel enacts a negotiation between "historical reality" and "a comprehensive view," assumes an active, meaning-making dialectic between text and reader (256). The novel is important for its power to enable "dialogue between subjectivities": "The realist novel matters because it explores ways past the individual mind" (79).[4] Whatever else it may also be, such a dialogue cannot avoid being an ethical project.

In line with Shaw's view, but with a different emphasis, is the important paradigm-shifting work of Caroline Levine. In *The Serious Pleasures of Suspense: Victorian Realism and Narrative Doubt*, Caroline Levine uncovers that Victorian thinking about realism emphasized realism's power to disrupt self-assurance. In the prevailing critical story also reviewed by Shaw, realism naturalizes dominant cultural myths and contains or dispels threats to the ideological status quo.[5] In contrast, Caroline Levine shows that in the early stage of Victorian thinking about realism in theoretical, critical, and literary texts, realism was offered as an experimental mode of testing hypotheses about the real and, often enough, finding them lacking. In the exemplary case of Ruskin, a realist aesthetic is "first and foremost a skeptical method" (12). This skepticism contains the seeds of political change, in that seeing what is really there liberates us from inherited mystifications: "Ruskin asks us to attend carefully to the otherness of nature in order to free ourselves both from the formulaic, repetitive habits of mind we have inherited from the past and from the growing tyranny of industrial labor" (13). In short, "The realist experiment is not about putting our faith in representation. It is about putting mimesis to the test" (12).[6]

In particular, suspense narratives inculcate skepticism about what one thinks one knows, requiring one to develop possible explanations for the phenomena given and then to rethink and remake those explanations when one's hypotheses turn out wrong. This readerly process engenders epistemological humility and deflates smug self-assurance. In this view, "closure does not so much dictate an arbitrary conclusion, as it compels us to recognize the otherness of the world, the ever-present possibility that the facts may refuse to validate our prejudices. Viewed in this light, suspense emerges as a profoundly subversive literary technique" (47).[7]

Caroline Levine's interest in the ethical implications of skepticism can be constructively linked to Andrew Miller's study *The Burdens of Perfection: On Ethics and Reading in Nineteenth-Century British Literature*. Miller begins by registering that "The period's literature was inescapably ethical in orientation: ethical in its form, its motivation, its aims, its tonality, its diction, its very style, ethical in ways that remain to be adequately assessed" (xi). Victorian skepticism, which is not so much doubt about God or religious matters as it is more generally doubt about what we can know about ourselves and others, gives rise to perfectionism, in which "doubt is not refuted ... but displaced or supplanted by a powerful attachment to someone who is found (in particular ways) to be exemplary" (xii). Victorian texts of all sorts, but especially the dramatic monologue and the realist novel, both represent such encounters among characters and perform them with their readers, including readers of the present day. Miller draws on the work of Stanley Cavell in perlocutionary discourse to examine how texts demand responses from their readers, how they are completed in the interpretative acts of readers and in the embodied acts that follow from those interpretations. Perfectionist prose is "successful only if it prompts a response" (17).

Like Caroline Levine, Miller dismisses claims that such an ethical project is hegemonic and oppressive, in service to reigning politico-economic forces. He points out that the response perfectionist texts elicit is not mere conformity, but is better described as resisting, conspiring, or completing the text. Perfectionism is a strategy found in radical as well as conservative politics, among poor as well as elite practitioners, and in feminist as well as patriarchal paradigms (12–13). A "new" sort of identity theory thus emerges:

> The individual who emerges in response to such an injunction is not the solitary subject of classical liberalism, cast against such imposing abstractions as the state or public opinion. Nor is it the

solitary self familiar from more recent cultural history, beating its wings against inescapable regimes of surveillance. Instead, moral perfectionism provides a complex, relational understanding of selfhood, one that does not reduce human contact to forms of domination and subjection. (15)

The implied reader of the Victorian texts Miller examines – the sort of reader the texts call into being – is therefore both politically and epistemologically capable of responding to the texts: she is both freer and more sophisticated than previous theorists allowed.

From Shaw we learn that Victorian realism is neither totalizing nor decentered; rather, it flexes between the poles of historical particularity and comprehensiveness. Realism is not entirely self-referential, nor does it naïvely purport to be transparently referential of external reality. Rather, it refers to structures and relationships in a historical moment to emphasize dynamic and contingent processes rather than fixed teleologies. It generates in readers the sorts of processes of cognitive and affective response that real life requires: in this sense it is also performative. From Caroline Levine we learn that realism is better understood as epistemologically subversive rather than epistemologically reassuring, and that that subversiveness carries ethical import, challenging readers to encounter alterity with openness and humility. From Andrew Miller we learn that realism is perlocutionary and ethical, not in ways that demand conformity, but in ways that awaken existential engagement.

All of these scholars, then, have recently argued for ways of understanding the relationship realist novels create between text and reader as performative and transformative, epistemological and ethical. The ethical import of fiction, on this understanding, is not reducible to crude didacticism in the sense of commending to the reader the choiceworthiness of particular moral actions, whether by positive or negative example, though in its Victorian forms it usually does not dispense with a guiding normativity of goodness. Rather, fiction is ethical insofar as it challenges self-absorption with alterity and complicates the existential stakes of moral commonplaces.[8] Moreover, the Victorian novel, at least in certain salient instances, does not so much lull readers into comfortable fictions in which they are encouraged to suspend critical thought; rather, it stiffens their consciousness of the limitations of conventional thinking and invites them to active interpretative practices in both cognitive and affective modes.⁹ If these scholars are right, the realist novel must be seen as eminently suited for the use of parabolic narrative strategies as described in my first chapter. Parables, too, confront the reader with a particular kind of alterity: the radical otherness of the kingdom of God, or what Ricoeur calls limit-experience. They make readers aware of the inadequacies of their default ethical and religious frameworks for genuinely transformative and transformed human life. They also induce skepticism – not in the sense of doubting the existence of God, but in the sense of destabilizing cultural idolatries. Parables inculcate skepticism about what people can know of God, God's plan, or themselves.

## Realism and Religion

However, even those who agree that realism's distinctive narrative techniques are performative, transformative, and disruptive might disagree that realism can be accommodated to religious, much less parabolic, ends. Indeed, for some it will seem that realism can be skeptical and countercultural only to the extent that it is resistant to discourses and norms that are recognizably religious and biblical. But this is to see religion as a static pole of cultural conservatism against which science, commerce, free-thinking, and other secularizing trends arrayed themselves in agonistic but ultimately successful conflict.

While this view does appear in some Victorian writing, and while it remains a critical commonplace in some circles, it is a view that is difficult to maintain in the face of recent scholarship about Victorian religion and culture. That scholarship chimes rather with Frances Power Cobbe's remark that "the secular life of the nation has been moulded by the religious creed, 'fashioned secretly' and growing together, acting and re-acting one on the other" (*Dawning Lights* 4). Recent research yields a picture of a society in which the religious and the secular were deeply interpenetrated, in which religion itself was multiform and richly controverted, and in which biblical texts and modes were put to an immense variety of uses. Frank Turner shows how Victorian studies has been poorly served by a secularization hypothesis blind to the vital religious culture – popular and elite and even scientific – of the period. He remarks, "That secularization of English and British culture occurred is true, but the occurrence was anything but inevitable, unproblematic, or systematically steady. The secularization thesis . . . left Victorian scholars unprepared to confront both the religious and the non-religious intellectual activities of the nineteenth century in all of their fulsome complexity" (35–36). Taking up Turner's call to "reexamine Victorian religion by probing its relationship to the secular areas of Victorian society" (24), Mark Knight and Emma Mason point to the "continual slippage between the sacred and the secular" in many social domains, including the "philosophical, scientific, medical, historical, and political" as well as of course the literary (3). Rebecca Styler finds in Victorian literary women "wider tendencies towards an 'incarnational' Christianity, in which the division between secular and sacred is blurred" (1). Timothy Larsen has recently shown that the Bible was central to the thinking and the rhetoric of Victorians, not only in the predictable instances of Methodists and Evangelicals but also in the cases of the Roman Catholic Cardinal Wiseman, the atheist Charles Bradlaugh, and the Unitarian Mary Carpenter. Radicals, freethinkers, and feminists were no less likely to appeal to scripture to bolster their social and political arguments than were clergymen of the Established Church.[10] It is now clear that the religious and the secular were overlapping rather than distinct spheres for the Victorians, and that the alleged disappearance and irrelevance of religious faith and practice in the face of modern science and social science has been greatly exaggerated.[11]

This view of religious activity and complexity invites a reconsideration of theories of realism that identify realism more or less with secularity, such as Georg Lukács's famous assertion that the novel is the "epic of a world abandoned by God" (Lukács 88) or Ian Watt's account of the novel's emergence out of "the conflict between spiritual and material values" in which secular values are "the dominant partner" (Watt 83). The central question for our purposes is whether the presence of the extraordinary in the ordinary necessarily renders a novel not realistic but fabulous. Put another way, does the novel's commitment to probability (granting that what is considered "probable" is another historical contingency) mean that the extraordinary cannot appear in it without putting the conventions of the novel under impossible strain?

Lukács's claims are not as problematic for my argument as they may first appear. Lukács does not mean that the novel cannot take shape around and within a religious world-ordering system, but only that the novel cannot take such a system as a prior, universal given, as the epic could. Lukács allows for any number of possible ordering structures, not excluding religious ones, and he does not assume that positing an ordering structure as contingent – as one choice among others – evacuates it of religious integrity in the interests of artistic purpose.[12] Watt, for his part, asserts that realism normally requires that "whatever the ends of the novelist may be, his means should be rigidly restricted to terrestrial characters and actions" (84). This normative description of the novel, however, does not exclude Ricoeur's idea of the extraordinary in the ordinary as it applies to parables, which do not, after all, entail the appearance of the supernatural or the immaterial on the page. With perhaps a single exception, the content of all Jesus's parables involves only actions entirely accessible to human beings:[13] no character in a parable performs or witnesses a miracle, a theophany, or other display of supernatural power. Ricoeur addresses the critique that his formulation of limit-experience is a "new form of supernaturalism" thus:

> [T]he eruption of the unheard in our discourse and in our experience constitutes precisely one dimension of our discourse and of our experience.... In th[e] expression – 'redescribes human experience' – we must emphasize both halves: what religious language does is to redescribe; what it redescribes is human experience. (127, emphasis in original)

The extraordinary in the ordinary is an extravagant human action – jaw-dropping in its self-effacement or generosity, or lethal in its assault on moral complacency, but not supernatural.[14]

In Victorian studies the strongest recent challenge to the potential for realism to have a religious, specifically a Christian, character appears in George Levine's *Realism, Ethics, and Secularism*. Levine acknowledges the religiosity of Victorian culture and the religious aspirations and affirmations of much Victorian fiction, but he argues that the "realist novel is predominantly a secular form, in which the implicit order of the world ... can only be achieved in worldly terms" (198). Not only is the novel "predominately" secular, but it is also "intrinsically secular" (212), "fundamentally secular" (200), and "fully secular" (229), though Levine also says that it is not "inevitably" secular (210). The various qualifications to the word "secular" are important because Levine seems to have in play simultaneously both a strong and a weak form of his argument: in the strong form, the novel is intrinsically, fundamentally, and fully secular; in the weak form, the novel "becomes a kind of battleground in which the developing conventions of the form itself often resist the pressures of the moral and sometimes explicitly religious energies that drive the novel" (212). In other words, the weak form allows for religious energies in the novel which are in tension with opposing energies, including the constraints of the genre; this is similar to Watt's position. But the strong form further maintains that religious energies are categorically out of place in the novel and only appear there, when they do, by the "strenuous" countervailing efforts of their authors (234). I don't think anyone would deny that the novel, when it touches on religion at all, intrinsically stages tensions that bear on religious practices and claims of religious truth, so if there is an argument, it would have to be with the strong version of Levine's formulation.

But in fact much of the problem with Levine's analysis derives from this very point of how completely "religious" a text has to be to count as "religious." A secular text, as Levine has it, can play host to religious energies and remain a "fully" and "fundamentally" secular text, but the reverse is apparently not true: a religious novel cannot play host to secular energies without "compromising" its religious aspirations (213). Levine in effect assumes that only the purely spiritual can be religious; if there is tension, which there always is in narrative, then the whole falls "willy-nilly" into the camp of the secular (229). This move requires Levine implicitly to posit as "religion" an impossibly pure and rarified realm of spiritual being, and thus to give over to "the secular" (an ever-expanding term for Levine, and one he declines to define) everything short of the supernatural, that is, everything material. So, for example, he claims that the form of the novel "largely through its fascination with material particularities, in effect blocks access to the transcendence it can nevertheless attempt to intimate" (217). And elsewhere, "The focus on money, in fact, is the firmest mark that realist fiction is fundamentally secular" (203). Notice the categorical exclusions: Material particularities, because they are material, block access to transcendence. Talk about money is categorically not religious talk.[15]

Such conclusions are very hard to square with Christianity, which rests on narratives of historical particularity and whose founder made money one of his chief subjects.[16] Levine's sense of Victorian religion seems to want to treat Christianity under the rubric of Gnosticism. Gnosticism, an early Christian heresy that has resurfaced from time to time in the West, teaches a total disassociation between the divine, which is wholly good and wholly spiritual, and the material, which is wholly evil.[17] Gnostics therefore deny that Jesus was an actual human being (God could not be joined to flesh) and require the actual or, more often, the gestural renunciation of material goods.[18] Corporeal life can only interfere with spiritual life, and the Gnostic's highest ambition is to escape the corporeal and achieve a purely ethereal existence. It was against early Gnosticism that the author of the epistle to the Colossians directed his scorn at those who bind believers to false ordinances barring the enjoyment of material goods (Col. 2:20-22). The orthodox doctrine of the incarnation, by contrast, insists that the earth is charged with the grandeur of God. In becoming flesh, the second person of the Trinity showed that material things participate in the goodness of God, though they, unlike God, are touched by the fall and are therefore more or less corrupted. So when Levine says that the novel form is intrinsically secular because "Fully fleshed narratives demand the kind of details that *embody* and *flesh out* ideas and faiths and inexplicable spiritual mysteries," his logic might hold for Gnosticism or perhaps for other religious traditions (210, my emphasis). But orthodox Christianity, obviously the dominant religion of Victorian England, has as its central "spiritual mystery" precisely the embodiment and enfleshing of the divine.[19]

The misconception of the relationship between the material and the spiritual in Christianity has consequences for the range of narrative possibilities that can operate with a Christian world view. Levine writes, "I focus then on the recognition implied in the novel ... that a fully naturalized world is one in which the Christian virtues that religious and Western culture had affirmed are, however desirable and admirable, only fragilely sustainable and easily corruptible or compromised" (213). This recognition, Levine indicates, is a counter-religious recognition. Yet the entire New Testament, with the possible exception of Revelation, bears abundant witness to Christian ideals being "only fragilely sustainable and easily corruptible or compromised." One thinks of the abrupt original ending of Mark, in which the women who have found Jesus's tomb empty are too startled and afraid to obey the angel's command to tell Jesus's followers what they have seen. Or Paul's reminders of how easy it is for a believer to become apostate as others have done. Or the ominous warning of the writer of Hebrews that he fears for his readers' stability in the faith due to their immaturity. In suggesting otherwise, Levine is expecting all Christian discourse to be of a certain triumphalistic and apocalyptic stamp. Much of it is, of course. But that posture is not a necessary feature of Christian narrative. In an anonymous article in *Blackwood's*, Margaret Oliphant easily assumes that she speaks a commonplace of Christian experience when she writes, "We all know ... that our Christianity in reality is more the perpetual struggle of a spirit resolved not to succumb, than of an ethereal victor, who daily raises himself higher and higher above all the motives and inducements of the world" ("Sermons" 737). Terry Eagleton suggests that Christian narrative, properly understood, avoids the triumphalistic and is therefore fully realistic: "It is by virtue of this impossible, stonily disenchanted realism, staring the Medusa's head of the monstrous, traumatic, obscene Real of human crucifixion full in the face, that some sort of resurrection may be possible" (27).

I do not of course mean to argue the opposite of Levine's formulation: that the novel is an intrinsically religious genre, or that the novel form somehow colludes towards religious structures and ideas "willy-nilly," despite authors' efforts to the contrary. I only argue that a genre that privileges probability and materiality does not for that reason necessarily exclude or compromise a Christian frame of reference. In fact, as we will see in the following chapter about Charlotte Yonge, the novel affords distinctive opportunities to an incarnational aesthetic, which believes that the divine is revealed in the material.

George Levine's sense of the incompatibility or mutual irrelevance of Christianity and realism receives some silent support from the other scholars I have been discussing. Shaw and Caroline Levine have a good bit to say about the implications of their theory of realism for narrative ethics, but nothing to say about the Christianity that doubtless lay behind the ethical intuitions of the authors they study. Shaw's intricate engagement with Erich Auerbach's *Mimesis* leaves the category of figural realism behind as it extrapolates the elements of a sound theory of realism from the shape or process rather than the content of Auerbach's discussions. Auerbach claimed that realism, defined as everyday events and ordinary people being treated as imbued with elevated or even cosmic significance, is essentially a narrative innovation enabled and first performed by the Hebrew and Christian scriptures; this claim does not figure in Shaw's discussion. Similarly, Shaw ignores the Christian typological roots of figural realism as Auerbach traces it in the history of Western literature ("Figura"). These omissions implicitly suggest that for Shaw the biblical and theological antecedents to realism have no continuing purchase in modernity. For his part, Andrew Miller acknowledges that evangelicalism was the strongest of the historical-ideological influences that made perfectionism a leading discursive mode in the nineteenth century. Most of his book, however, plays down that influence, focusing rather on the Habermasian view that moderns were forced to generate their ethics out of their own resources (20–21, 24). In spite of their obvious overlap, the ethical turn and the religious turn in literary and cultural studies have not been brought together, at least in Victorian studies.[20] This disconnect would have been incomprehensible to the Victorians themselves: Matthew Arnold famously said that the purview of religion is conduct, and that conduct is at least three-fourths of life (Arnold 14).[21]

George Levine is right thus far: a realist novel cannot directly portray the fullness of limit-experience, or the kingdom of God. But it can do something much like what Jesus's parables do: it can use particular sets of human relationships and responses to show gesturally or sometimes metaphorically what "human reality in its wholeness" might look like in particular instances (Ricoeur 127). It can show one or more people responding to an ordinary situation in an extraordinary way, a way that is fully on the plane of human action but which challenges ordinary ideas about, for example, how many times one can forgive another, or about whether people can change for the better. I am not, of course, claiming that every positive or "redemptive" ending makes a parable or that every morally idealized character expresses a particularly Christian affirmation. But in texts that make extensive use of plots, characters, and reversals borrowed from Jesus's parables, we may fairly look for both the sophisticated narrative strategies that give parables their existential potency and for portrayals of limit-experience: moments of human action that partake of transcendence and that suggest elements of what a perfected human existence might look like or might enable.

The strongest instance of these parabolic elements is found, not surprisingly, in the fiction of Charlotte Yonge. Working out of a thoroughly articulated theological paradigm of Christian orthodoxy, Yonge's retelling of the parable of the Pharisee and the publican in *The Heir of Redclyffe* (1853) is self-conscious of its claims to represent perfected human experience and to make that experience particularly confrontational to the reader through the use of parabolic reversal. *The Heir of Redclyffe* thus clicks snugly into place all the components of parable and literature I have been discussing: Yonge's retelling becomes not only a modernizing reinterpretation but also a renewed encounter with the parable's confrontational effect, which is achieved by the eruption of extravagant forgiveness and repentance into an otherwise realistic narrative saturated with materiality. The snug fit is facilitated by Yonge's thoroughgoing identification with Anglo-Catholicism, which offered her a distinctive aesthetic theory based on the doctrine of reserve, which is itself based partly on the operation of the parables in the synoptic gospels.

In the case of Margaret Oliphant, the guiding theological principles are less precisely articulated and less visible. Nonetheless, she too reworks parabolic material in ways that point towards a redescription of human existence. In her repeated engagements with the parable of the prodigal son, she found a template that allowed her to express her deeply felt struggle with the problematic of divine justice and forgiveness. Particularly in *The Perpetual Curate* (1864), the parable of the prodigal son forms an important subtext through which she frames not only key aspects of character development but also her anguished protest against undeserved human suffering. In some of her later fiction, the parable took on added significance for her as the bereaved mother of two disappointing sons. My reading draws on the biographical events that colored Oliphant's attitudes and responses to Christianity and its claims of truth, not to explain these attitudes away, but rather to focus critical attention on the complex formal and thematic engagement with serious theological questions that appears even in her comic fiction.

Unlike Yonge and Oliphant, Charles Dickens was widely identified as a parabolist by readers in his own time as well as ours. Yet the opportunities afforded by this study for a heightened theoretical consciousness of parable allow such descriptions to be more finely sifted. Dickens's "parables" are often taken to mean merely narratives with a forceful ethical import, but I suggest that understanding the relationship of his novels to the parables reframes key critical problems. In *Our Mutual Friend* (1865), the stewardship parables, particularly the parable of the wise and foolish steward, become a vital intertext for unraveling the multiple convoluted plots to find the novel's ethical and theological center of gravity. Rather than asking whether the novel's dark vision of London as a trash-heap is adequately answered by its redemptive but understated ending, the background intertext of the stewardship parables points towards a vision in which the normative mode of human life is one of suspended expectation for a present, yet unrealized, eschaton.

Each of these authors uses a gesture of extravagance to oppose a different shortcoming in the period's conventional religious or moral framework. Yonge's target is a Pharisaical moral complacency which assumes that outward respectability is adequate for the Christian. However, she extends the moral burden from the characters *in* the text to the readers *of* the text in a double reversal which challenges the reader's willingness to embrace the extravagance that grants repentance and redemption even to the self-righteous villain of the novel. The epistemological humility and moral strenuousness suggested in this plot transformation are expressive of similar sentiments found in the nonfiction writing of Yonge's Oxford Movement colleagues.

Oliphant's patterns of praise and blame are less stark than Yonge's, but she too offers a challenge to conventional religious and moral ideas. In fact her challenge is twofold: she disdains the cherished Victorian cult of domesticity by rewriting the parable of the prodigal son so as to desentimentalize the actions of both the prodigal and the father. At the same time, Oliphant's reinscriptions of the parable confront easy platitudes about divine justice. Her plots not only expose the inadequacy of consoling assumptions that human suffering can be explained with reference to human merit or demerit, but they also echo the deeply felt struggle with this question expressed in Oliphant's other writing. Like the parable she repeatedly used to come to terms with this quandary, Oliphant's fiction is both destabilizing and affirmative, and it resists easy closure.

Dickens's multifarious attacks on the moral inadequacies of his society and its leaders are well known. In *Our Mutual Friend* as elsewhere, he particularly targets the materialism that reduces people to objects and money to a tool of self-aggrandizement. Characters who crave and hoard money, including Old Harmon, Silas Wegg, and Fascination Fledgeby, use it to tyrannize over others and find themselves enslaved by it to their own injury. Against them is arrayed a contrasting set of characters who hold their possessions in a posture of stewardship, including Mr. and Mrs. Boffin, John Harmon, and Riah. These characters not only experience freedom from the corrupting power of money but also are able to liberate others, such as Bella. The literal extravagance of the Boffins, who are always looking to transfer their fortune to John rather than hold onto it, and of John, who goes to great lengths to avoid gaining possession of the same fortune, shows that a Christian model of stewardship, as against an exclusively capitalistic model of material self-interest, preserves humane values as well as wealth. Like Yonge and Oliphant, Dickens uses the narrative strategy of reversal to draw the reader into the gap portrayed between the conventional political economy that enslaves and the financial and relational extravagance that liberates.

In these chapters, I enter the critical conversation on each author in different places. Yonge's religious positions are fairly clear and well understood, but what is not as well understood is how her fiction participates in those positions both aesthetically and theologically. Hence Chapter 3 makes primarily an argument about Yonge's astute use of parable form and strategy to write a novel that is both performative and perlocutionary, but also reserved in the Tractarian sense. By contrast, Oliphant's religious views have been much overlooked and their relevance to her fiction has hardly been touched. So, Chapter 4 makes a background case for the importance of religion to Oliphant on its way to exploring her use of the narrative potentialities of parable. The embarrassment of critical riches that attends the study of Dickens includes much about his use of scripture and about his religious views. Yet the particular focus on the ways parables work to redescribe human experience helps to clarify the stakes of the persistent tendency of critics to offer intuitive judgments about the adequacy of Dickens's positive endings. Taken together, these readings demonstrate fresh possibilities for understanding extrabiblical parables and shed new light on the Victorians' aesthetic and theological engagement with Christian texts and teachings.

# 3

# "The Parable of Actual Life": Charlotte Yonge's *The Heir of Redclyffe*

Charlotte Yonge's 1890 story "The Price of Blood" is a Christian rewrite of the Damon and Pythias legend. Set in fourth-century Gaul, the conflict arises from tensions between an orthodox Christian community and nearby Goth heretics; the young men of both sides are overly prone to settle disagreements by violence, often leading to death. When a Christian young man kills a Goth in a fight, the Goths demand payment by blood, but the murderer's friend surreptitiously offers himself in his place. When the guilty man realizes this has been done, he desperately races to the place of execution to forestall his friend's sacrifice, while the friend urges that the execution be carried out promptly before the guilty man can arrive. Seeing this heroic love and loyalty between friends, a noble young Goth is converted to orthodoxy on the spot. A benign old bishop, looking on, points the moral for the young readers: "Thus hath the parable of actual life led this zealous but half-taught youth to enter into the higher truth" (46).[1]

This line suggests something of Yonge's sense of the nature and potentiality of parable. Parables occur in "actual life"; they are the ordinary transposed into something extraordinary by a special kind of spiritual vision. Moreover, parables are instructive not so much cognitively as viscerally. The story played out in the presence of the young Goth is more persuasive than any expository or discursive exercise could be. Furthermore, that persuasiveness is most effective on the "zealous but half-taught." That is, parables work most powerfully on those who desire to be faithful to God but who are only partially instructed in what God requires. These are people who are receptive to the teachings God may bring them in "actual life," even or perhaps especially when those teachings come by surprise, but who have certain spiritual blind spots or habits of worldly thought that require correction. A declared rebel against God or a person completely ignorant of Christian teaching will not perceive the lesson hidden in the "parable of actual life."

This chapter will argue that Charlotte Yonge's best-known novel, *The Heir of Redclyffe* (1853), is, in its way, a "parable of actual life," using realism to bring Christian "higher truth" home, literally as well as figuratively, to the massive novel-reading public of the mid-nineteenth century. *The Heir of Redclyffe* is a retelling of the parable of the Pharisee and the publican from Luke 18, but it is also a parable in its own right, as it reconfigures the types from the biblical parable in order to deliver a similarly disruptive, even offensive, message of moral confrontation to readers. The parabolic qualities of *The Heir of Redclyffe* constitute a sophisticated engagement with distinctive Tractarian principles of aesthetic and hermeneutic theory, including the doctrine of reserve and the related Tractarian view of parables.

Charlotte Yonge (1823–1901) was the leading novelist of the Oxford Movement. Parishioner and friend of John Keble, Yonge viewed her prolific writing career as an "instrument for popularising Church views" (Dennis 125). Her early success *The Heir of Redclyffe*, by far the most popular and enduring of her more than one hundred works of fiction, was warmly admired by Henry James and William Morris. Yonge's conservative ideology apparently kept her out of the mainstream of the feminist recovery of minor women writers, and she has been largely neglected until quite recently.

The perennial problem for critics of Yonge is the relationship of her realism to her didacticism. While admiring her complex psychological portraits and detailed descriptions of quotidian family life, readers since her own time have tended to fault her improbable manipulation of plot to reinforce her dogmatic aims.[2] Yonge's detractors dismiss her on these grounds.[3] Yonge's reluctant admirers (and most of her admirers are at least somewhat reluctant) are frequently seen to rejoice that Yonge's realism generally overcomes her dogmatism, that her interesting characters refuse to be straitjacketed according to predetermined Tractarian notions.[4]

Many readers see only random improbabilities intruding as flaws into otherwise realistic fiction, but more perceptive readers have noticed coherent patterns that control the novels' nonrealist elements within a logic of their own. Kim Wheatley's analysis of the improbabilities of the plot in *The Clever Woman of the Family* (1865) reveals that the novel "works simultaneously on two levels: as a set of [realist] psychological portraits and as a simple moral fable" in which verisimilitude is rightly left to the side (909). Similarly, *The Heir of Redclyffe* has long been appreciated as a hybrid of realism and romance. Catherine Sandbach-Dahlström helpfully reads the novel in these terms without insisting on seeing either genre as necessarily detrimental to the other. In *Heir* the realist plot, which has Philip and Laura as its hero and heroine, runs alongside the romance plot of Guy and Amy until the final section.

For Gavin Budge, the operative terms are rather realism and typology. Budge shows that the modern assumption that didacticism and realism are incompatible – that didactic purpose mars artistic integrity – is far from being a given in the nineteenth century, when aesthetic and ethical theory were often seen as related to each other. Budge's analysis of contemporaneous aesthetic theory, including that of Yonge's mentor and neighbor John Keble, shows that religious typology was construed as part of the real of the created order, not foisted upon the real by ingenious interpretations. (In addition to being one of the three leading lights of the Oxford Movement, Keble was also at one time the Professor of English Poetry at Oxford, and his *Lectures on Poetry* were highly influential on the aesthetic theory of his generation.[5]) Budge reads *Heir* typologically as an allegory of the nineteenth-century Everyman's progress through rational utilitarianism to intuitive faithfulness, concluding that "[f]rom Yonge's point of view, ... realism and typology cannot be separated ... : typological significance is implicit in the form of the novel itself, as an attempt to generalize about human experience in language" (217).[6]

Budge's reading usefully allows us to circumvent the need to see realism and didacticism as competing for control of the text, but I find that his and Sandbach-Dahlström's discussions of genre and tropic techniques do not do full justice to either Yonge's didactic or artistic achievement in *The Heir of Redclyffe*. Such justice can only be done by taking account of how the book not only represents moral progress but also challenges the reader's own moral state. That challenge, I will show, is contained in the book's emotional effect on the reader. As Nicola Diane Thompson observed, "critics tend to focus their comments on the effects *The Heir of Redclyffe* has on its readers, rather than on the work's intrinsic literary qualities, perhaps partly in response to the novel's religious elements" (97). This trend has not greatly abated: the recent sophisticated articles of Talia Schaffer, for example, take as their starting preoccupation the "powerful [emotional] reactions – and particularly the consistent impulse to express them" seen in many Yonge critics, including Schaffer herself ("Magnum Bonum" 246). In the case of *The Heir of Redclyffe* at least, I suggest that these reactions are not incidental but intrinsic to the design of the novel. In that light I propose that the genre best suited to describe the peculiar moral force of Yonge's realism is parable. In fact this novel's distinctive reversals enact all the elements of parabolic narrative strategy we have seen in the previous chapters. The novel stages a gap between the ordinary and the extraordinary, or limit-experience, by the use of extravagance in the plot, and the effect is to disorient the reader's default moral paradigm in order to suggest the possibility for reorientation.

Aside from overall enjoyment of the novel and its characters, the affective reaction to *The Heir of Redclyffe* that has been most consistently expressed is a strong *dis*like of the novel's ending, in which Yonge prolongs the tale well beyond the death of the hero (Guy) to narrate the repentance of the anti-hero (Philip). As we will see, Yonge had ample warning of this negative response in the views of her own family and friends when they read the book in manuscript. I suggest that Yonge's choice of an ending – and readers' hostile and uncomprehending reactions to it – becomes intelligible when we view the novel as a parable. In this light, Yonge's aim of illustrating moral exemplarity in the characters is secondary to her aim of challenging the reader's own moral state, precisely in the book's affront to the reader's sympathies. My reading will show that *Heir* not only retells the parable of the Pharisee and the publican, but also becomes a potent Victorian parable.[7] It does so by reversing the reversal of the parable in order to deliver to the reader something like the startling effect that Jesus's parable delivered to its original audiences. Evidence for the success of this effect, I argue, is found in the overwhelmingly negative reaction of readers to the book's ending.

My first section below will link Yonge's project to the particular resonances of parables – and of this parable – in Tractarian thinking. In the second section I trace the correspondences between *Heir* and the parable of the Pharisee and the publican. Finally, my consideration of the ending and of readers' reactions to it will show how this novel achieves the parabolic quality of challenging the reader's assumptions about who does and does not enjoy divine favor.

*****

Perhaps because Yonge strikes us today as quaint and reactionary in her gender and class politics, most critics until quite recently have assumed that she is best explained as lamentably captive to conventional Victorian ideology.[8] Gavin Budge does much to debunk this reading in his recent *Charlotte M. Yonge: Religion, Feminism and Realism in the Victorian Novel*, arguing not only for Yonge's self-consciousness as an author but also for her counter-cultural stance on key social and religious issues. This correction is based on the fact that Tractarianism was never in the mainstream of Victorian religious thought, but remained in the position of an embattled minority (62). Budge shows that "Tractarians such as Yonge engaged in consciousness-raising whose effect was to make them question Victorian social assumptions," although many critical readings of Yonge "neglect the critical and psychologically self-aware perspective on Victorian culture for which Yonge is indebted to Tractarianism" (11–12).

This view of Yonge's social and artistic milieu suggests parallels with what we have seen of the nature and effect of parables. Parables are faithful to the religious tradition within which they arise, yet they aggressively challenge the reduction or deformation of that tradition into conventional morality or religious platitudes. As we have seen, parables not only privilege but even demand a reading practice that entails interpretation and participation. The dominant view of Yonge as merely didactic, telling stories that reinforce received Victorian moral and social conventions, would not allow for the readerly engagement or social confrontation characteristic of parables. But as Budge shows, Yonge conceived that moral choice follows from a person's prior perspective on that choice, and that one's perspective in turn follows from the set of associations one has formed.[9] In this view, novels are not moral because they recommend virtue and condemn vice in any narrowly didactic way, but rather because they draw the reader into the process of forming associations that enable accurate judgment of the ethical stakes in any particular decision (*Charlotte M. Yonge* 87–89). This essentially hermeneutic exercise educates the reader in the right interpretation of character and circumstance: "[F]ar from being crudely 'didactic' in the sense of asserting moral judgments that are presumed to be applicable in all circumstances, Yonge's novels are designed to act as occasions for the reader to reflect on the process of interpretation by which they arrive at the moral judgments which they apply to the text" (161). Budge further discusses "those critical and ironic elements in Yonge's writing the experience of which is reliant on the reader's willingness to play an active interpretative role, and which have often been neglected by critics who assume that Yonge's religious commitment necessarily implies a dogmatic denial of interpretative freedom to the reader" (46). In this view, Yonge problematizes the very questions of epistemology and ethics that most critics have assumed she treats as givens.

Budge's insights put Yonge in the stream of Victorian realism that Andrew Miller and Caroline Levine have shown to be preoccupied with testing what is true, ontologically and ethically. Both Levine and Miller, in different ways, show that realism does not work to reassure the reader of the truth of her ideological presuppositions, but rather to guide the reader through a process of testing what she thinks she knows against what is there. Realism is a skeptical genre that demands, or even creates, a skeptical reader. It may seem odd to associate Yonge with skepticism in any sense, but this is precisely the association Andrew Miller makes with John Henry Newman. For Newman, a serious threat to the faithfulness of Victorian Christians was "knowingness" or the smug confidence that we already know who we are and what is the reality of our moral state. Newman described knowingness as an "evil crust" that prevents the discovery and therefore the repudiation of sins that survive as blind spots (qtd. in Miller, *Burdens* 145). Newman urged Christians to bring to bear skepticism of themselves and of their moral achievements in order to escape the insidious sin of self-righteousness.[10]

Miller shows that the devoutly religious person is indeed skeptical, but that skepticism is directed at himself rather than at religious tradition or authority (*Burdens* 143–146).

Parables, as we have seen, also work to destabilize the condition Newman calls "knowingness." Tractarian thought about parables is of a piece with the movement's overall theological and aesthetic affinities. According to the Tractarian doctrine of reserve as articulated in John Keble's *Lectures on Poetry*, what religion and literature have in common is that both conceal their meaning as well as reveal it, or conceal it while revealing it.[11] Sacred truths, whether in scripture, liturgy, or literature, are veiled in indirect discourses that can only be penetrated by readers whose "devotion be such as leads [them] to take zealous pains to search [truth] out" (Keble 482). The reader will enter into the meaning of the text to a degree proportionate to his or her moral preparation: "[I]t is a certain state of the heart which could alone receive [instruction] in the sense implied" (Williams 7). In Tract 80, written by cleric Isaac Williams as an apology for the doctrine of reserve, Jesus's parables are described as a paradigmatic instance of this phenomenon. In parables, "[T]he most spiritual and heavenly precepts were thus left to the rude and rough world, so that the veil of the figure might still be over them, though disclosing its import to any attentive and thoughtful person" (10). Those who bring to a parable a reverent and repentant disposition will understand its message, while resistant readers – those seeking to master the text rather than be mastered by it – will be kept outside the meaning (Williams 8–11). Yonge scrupulously observed this doctrine in various ways, including avoiding the use of specific sacred words in her fiction, depicting characters whose reverence is powerful but largely inarticulate, and refraining from explicit doctrinal discussion while yet encoding doctrine in a veiled or implicit fashion in her narratives.[12] Given Yonge's beliefs that she should write fiction in conformity with the doctrine of reserve, and that Jesus used parables as an originary instance of the doctrine, it is a very small step for Yonge to imagine her novels as parabolic in function, technique, and effect.

Yonge's participation in Tractarian thought and practice concerns not only the theory of parables generally, but also specific treatments of the parable of the Pharisee and the publican. This parable accorded well with the Tractarians' predilection towards a strenuous goodness that does not settle for merely conventional or respectable morality. In Jesus's parable in Luke 18, the Pharisee lifts his eyes to heaven and thanks God that he is not a sinner "as other men are, extortioners, unjust, adulterers, or even as this publican" (18:11). He then reminds God of his moral achievements of tithing and fasting. The publican, for his part, "would not lift up so much as his eyes unto heaven, but smote upon his breast, saying, God be merciful to me, a sinner" (18:13). The Pharisee's moral complacency, if it is slightly offensive, is at least well-founded in his demonstrable acts of piety. The publican's self-abnegation is equally what can be expected of a notorious sinner who bothers to come to the Temple at all. The reversal, then, lies in the concluding remark of Jesus: that the publican "went down to his house justified rather than the other: for every one that exalteth himself shall be abased; and he that humbleth himself shall be exalted" (18:14). Divine favor is extravagantly and unexpectedly offered to the sinner and withheld from the (seeming) righteous.

Far from being a simple good vs. bad case study in morality, the parable posits a radical reversal of what Harrison calls "everyday morality." The extortionary tax-collector is justified; the spotless Law-abiding Pharisee is not. Joachim Jeremias notes, "Such a conclusion must have utterly overwhelmed its hearers" (114). The worldly real is suspended in the face of the transcendent real as Jesus teaches that those who seem the farthest from the kingdom are actually the nearest, and those who seem nearest are farthest. This is why Geraint Vaughan Jones describes this parable as "deadly in [its] effect and deliberately offensive in [its] intention" (111). As in many parables, the extravagance appears in a reversal that subverts the reader's expectations of what is real in ordinary human experience (God approves of people who keep all the rules) with an alternate vision of what is real from the perspective of the gospel (God responds in love to people who seek God in humility and penitence). In the former, God is conscripted to bolster human systems of social and religious control, while in the latter, God breaks apart those systems to affirm the value and redeemability of every person. This juxtaposition, we recall from Chapter 1, is what Ricoeur calls a redescription of human experience, and it is made possible precisely by the unexpected appearance of the extraordinary in the midst of the ordinary.

For the Tractarians, the lesson of Jesus's opposition to conventional religiosity had a great deal of current purchase. Both

John Henry Newman and E. B. Pusey claimed that the Victorian cult of respectability was a version of Pharisaism and should be opposed by true Christians. Newman's Anglican sermons are peppered with admonitions against the complacent belief that one merits God's favor by conformity to everyday morality. The ordinary level of externally visible honesty, sexual probity, and social affability are, to Newman, mere pagan self-interest, since the nominally Christian middle-class Victorian culture rewards such so-called virtue. Rather, Newman insists, truly Christian virtue consists in a radical obedience to Scripture that "forc[es] you past the fear of men, and the usages of society, and the persuasions of interest" (48). Elsewhere he declares that conforming merely to popular morality "bring[s] in its train a selfish temperance, a selfish peaceableness, a selfish benevolence, the morality of expedience" that, in its "*appearance* of obedience" leaves one with "no hope of salvation" (25, 27, emphasis in original). Crucially, Pharisaism, or prideful self-righteousness arising from scrupulous conformity to conventional morality, is the precise moral failure against which so many of Jesus's parables are directed, including the parables of the prodigal son, the Good Samaritan, and the vineyard owner. Pharisaism is especially difficult to challenge, since its essence is the self-complacency that is all but immune to reproach. What makes parables effective against Pharisaism is the way they lead unsuspecting readers into the recognition of their sin, as the prophet Nathan did with King David. According to Newman, the Christian avoids Pharisaism by remaining skeptical of his own moral judgments, especially of himself; parables, which disrupt one's unexamined assumptions of what constitutes acceptable morality, induce such skepticism.

For his part, Pusey called Pharisaism "the central failure of this day," and insisted that "we all have more or less of the Pharisee clinging to us; for it presses in upon us through all the habits and ways of our times . . . and if we are not conscious of some Pharisaism, it is the Pharisaism itself which blinds us" (8, 16). In his Ash Wednesday sermon "Our Pharisaism," Pusey said, "[I]f we detested or despised [the Pharisee], as being in any way our inferior, . . . we should have arrived at out-Pharisee-ing the Pharisee" (1). Pusey's point is that precisely to the extent that one uses this parable to condemn the other, whom one labels "Pharisee," one becomes the target of the parable. The only sinless application of this parable, therefore, is to see oneself as the Pharisee; that act of seeing paradoxically makes one into the publican, asking pardon for one's manifest and hidden sins.[13]

In a similar vein, Archbishop Richard Trench, whom Yonge admired, claimed that Jesus directed the parable not at the Pharisees but at the "disciple, one already having made some little progress in the school of Christ, yet in danger, *as we are all in danger*, of falling back into pharisaic sins." Such a disciple "would only need his sin to be plainly shown to him, and he would start back at its deformity; he would recognize the latent Pharisee in himself, and tremble and repent" (502–503, emphasis added).[14] Trench exhorts his readers not to see the Pharisee as the other, but as themselves, and he points out the remedy to be the humble penitence of the publican.

Yonge puts this view of the parable to work in *Heir*. In Yonge's earliest plans for the book, the binary structure used in the parable is the foundation of her elaborate plot: she wrote that there were "two characters she wanted to see brought out in a story – namely, the essentially contrite and the self-satisfied." Yonge further noted that "Good men ... were in most of the books of the day ..., whereas the 'penitence of the saints' was unattempted" (*Musings* xxix). In keeping with her project of exemplarity, Yonge presents the negative model of the Pharisee (Philip Morville) and the positive alternative: the person who combines the conscientiousness of the Pharisee with the penitence of the publican (Sir Guy Morville, the heir of Redclyffe).

But Yonge's parable is not merely exemplary, any more than Jesus's is. It is also, in its way, subversive of conventional morality even as it extravagantly subverts expectations about realism. This subversion occurs in the novel's ending: if the reversal of the parable is that even a publican who repents can be justified, the double reversal of the novel is that even a *Pharisee* who repents can be justified. Crucially, however, the novel exposes not only the Pharisaism of Philip, but also that of the reader who is eager to condemn Philip. In demanding the reader's transferal of sympathy from the saintly Guy to the despicable Philip, the text confronts the reader with his or her own Pharisaism much like the Lukan parable does. Yonge's reader, like Trench's, is asked to "recognize the latent Pharisee in himself, and tremble and repent." Yonge knows that her biblically informed readers will expect the contrite man, however sinful, to be the hero, and the Pharisiaical man, however upright, to be the villain. This favoring of the publican over the Pharisee was, for the Victorian public, a platitude; to use Ricoeur's terms, it is like a stale metaphor that no longer excites the imagination or engenders new insight. After seeming to mislead the reader briefly at the very beginning, Yonge plays to that conventional expectation for the bulk of the novel. However, the unexpected double reversal restores the parable's subversive effect with the conversion of the Pharisee, which has its biblical precedent not in Jesus's parable but rather in the "parable of actual life" of the apostle Paul. This conversion, engendered out of the limit-experience of Guy's saintliness, ultimately challenges the Pharisaism of the reader via Yonge's own parable of actual life.

\*\*\*\*\*

Pharisaism, in the Victorian context, denoted not so much the sect of Judaism blamed in the gospels for its hypocrisy and persecution of Jesus; rather the word served as a generalized term of opprobrium usually directed by Christians against co-religionists whom they regarded as hypocritical. Pharisaism is often seen as synonymous with hypocrisy, but the words are not necessarily coterminous. The difference can be seen by contrasting Philip to such stock hypocrite-villains in Victorian fiction as Dickens's Mr. Chadband or Charlotte Brontë's Mr. Brocklehurst. The gap between their professions and their actions is so very egregious as to be treated as a broad joke or broad outrage. In the case of the "pure" Pharisee, however, particularly in the instance of the parable of the Pharisee and the publican which Yonge is retelling, there is little or no visible incongruity between profession and conduct. E. B. Pusey's sermon makes this point about Pharisaism and hypocrisy particularly clear: "Many Pharisees were hypocrites, our Lord tells us. He does not say so of *him*. We have only to take his character, as our Lord gives it" (Pusey 3–4, emphasis in original). Pusey's target is not the relatively obvious one of people who pretend to be good but are not, but rather the subtler problem of people, like Philip, whose real moral uprightness leads them to the damnable condition of self-righteousness.

That this distinction was clear to Yonge can be seen by looking at other books and characters in which Pharisaism and hypocrisy are distinguished. In *The Clever Woman of the Family*, the self-complacent Rachel has not a shadow of hypocrisy – she earnestly and sincerely believes and does everything she claims to believe and do. The hypocrite Bessie of that novel, who hides her peccadilloes from others to escape social censure for them, does not exhibit any symptom of self-righteousness. Theodora of *Heartsease*, like Rachel of *The Clever Woman of the Family*, is a Pharisee without being a hypocrite. Flora of *The Daisy Chain* is an instance of both: she combines "complacent self-satisfaction" with a religious life that is merely "mechanical" (ch. 20).

Philip's Pharisaism is such that his moral failure only becomes evident when he is brought into contact with his cousin Guy. This contact occurs through the Edmonstone family, consisting of a father and mother, an adult son Charlie who is crippled, and three daughters: Laura and Amy, approaching marriageable age, and the younger Charlotte. Philip's goodness is not feigned, and his adherence to Church teaching is not, as has been claimed, "superficial" (Dennis 57–58).[15] Like the Pharisee in the parable, he consistently observes correct and honorable behavior, even to his own cost. The high regard for Philip expressed by the steady and serious Laura, the warm and principled Mrs. Edmonstone, and Philip's regimental colleagues and their families clearly establishes him as a "pattern" young man. A typical remark by his colonel's wife praises Philip's "excellent judgment, kindness of heart, and power of leading to the right course" (52). Guy himself is particularly affected by the story of Philip's noble sacrifice of a promising academic career to enter the army so as to maintain his sister in their childhood home. Only Charlie is prone to detract, but his habitual petulance and caustic tone, together with his evident jealousy of the attention given to Philip, compromise his credibility as a judge of Philip's character. Even Philip's failure to appreciate Guy could be taken as meritorious at first, as it seems to derive from a principled refusal to be charmed by superficial qualities. Not until the fourth chapter does Philip's unacknowledged jealousy and spitefulness manifest itself in needlessly provoking behavior toward his younger and more fortunate cousin. Even then, it is the intangibles that offend. Philip's moral failure, being covert like that of the Pharisee, can only be detected in his "veiled assumption of superiority" (48): his conduct, principles, and even his manners are irreproachable.

This early misdirection of the reader's judgment appears to have been anticipated, if not intended, by Yonge. As she began the book,

Yonge wrote to her friend Marianne Dyson, "On reading my first chapter I doubt whether Philip will not strike those who do not know him as intended for the perfect hero; I rather hope he will, and as one of those perfect heroes whom nobody likes" (Coleridge 175).[16] A little later she added, "Mamma says people will think [Philip] is the good one to be rewarded, and Guy the bad one punished. I say if stupid people really think so, it will be just what I should like, for it would be very like the different morals caught by different people from real life" (Coleridge 177). After the first few chapters, no one could mistake Philip's identity as "the bad one," but Yonge's willingness for her readers' sympathy to be misled shows that she is intentional not only about the reversals embedded in the narrative, but also about challenging readers' facile notions of the hermeneutics of character. The first reversal occurs as the reader is made to recognize that the apparently upright Philip is actually the novel's villain.

Again and again we see Philip's scrupulous honesty working alongside his self-deception to produce a moral blindness that is the more dangerous for being partially examined. Philip's very determination to be perfectly honest and fair-minded convinces him that he cannot be mistaken or prejudiced. His criticisms of Guy's character are often accompanied by such apparently reasonable caveats as "I am not condemning him; I wish to be perfectly just; all I say is, that I do not trust him till I have seen him tried" (35). Another time he explains his galling behavior thus: "It may be painful to ourselves, and irritating to [Guy], but depend upon it, it is the proof of friendship" (89). On the strength of that assurance of disinterestedness Philip becomes less and less capable of doing Guy justice. Philip descends to increasingly corrupt behavior driven by his very confidence in his own perfection and purity of motive.

Significantly, Philip's suspicions of Guy are bolstered by appeals to conventional realist psychology. Philip is quick to put a negative construction on Guy's impulsive acts of self-restraint (such as giving up hunting and not going to the regimental ball) based on Philip's ideas of human nature: "Philip, firm in his preconceived idea of [Guy's] character, and *his own knowledge of mankind*, was persuaded that he had imputed the true motive" (73, emphasis added). In other words, he insists on judging Guy by the standard of realism, and thereby attributes to him the feelings of a slighted lover or of wounded pride. "It is caprice or temper," Philip declares of Guy's absence from the ball, dismissing as "incredible!" Guy's own explanation of self-discipline (131). Charlie describes this mistake later when he says, "I knew it would come out later that [Guy] had only been so much better than other people that nobody could believe it" (334). The limitations of what Philip can believe to be "real" highlight his alienation from the self-transcending values heralded in Jesus's parables.

At first Philip merely provokes Guy's anger and enjoys the uncharitable self-satisfaction of seeing his suspicions of Guy's hasty temper fulfilled. But later Philip proceeds to active persecution by pouncing on flimsy and rumored evidence that Guy has gambled. Philip persuades Mr. Edmonstone to bar Guy from the Edmonstone home, where he has lived since the death of his grandfather at the beginning of the novel, and to call off the engagement between Guy and Amy. For many months, until Mr. Edmonstone is brought to his senses by Guy's heroic rescue of some shipwrecked sailors in a storm, Guy endures a dark night of the soul as he forgives Philip's calumny, repents of his hasty words against Philip and Mr. Edmonstone, and resigns his future happiness to God.

In Philip's relationship with Laura as well, the impossibility of seeing himself as at fault leads Philip into what the narrator calls "the first occasion that he had ever actually swerved from the path of right" (120). His premature avowal of love with Laura, immediately cloaked in rigorous secrecy, is regarded by Yonge as a "betray[al] of confidence" of Laura's parents (120). It is fitting that Philip's first clearly wrong action is a secret one. As he justifies this breach of confidence to himself and to Laura, it is clear that his problem is that he is so used to being right, and so used to dictating the right to others, that he cannot imagine being wrong himself. This same habit of mind is seen in the way he disdains to look for evidence that would exonerate Guy and even refuses to credit the exculpating evidence he is given, because "it made no difference in his real opinion" (257). Convinced in his own mind, and utterly unable to imagine being mistaken, Philip persists in absurd constructions of facts in order to make them agree with his foregone conclusion. Laura similarly bears out Charlie's prediction that "Laura was so much too wise for one of her age, that nature would some day take her revenge, and make her do something very foolish" (424). In other words, her certainty of right – her habit of a righteousness needing no repentance – is precisely what leads her wrong.

Much later, after Guy's death, Philip reflects, "It had been his bane that he had been always too sensible to betray outwardly his self-conceit, in any form that could lead to its being noticed" (521). The interiority of his sin is far more dangerous to his spiritual condition because it obviates the continual repentance that alone makes one justified before God according to the parable. The description of the Pharisee in Pusey's sermon could be taken for a sketch of Philip himself:

> He, and we too often dwell on any good [qualities] we think we have; we tacitly lay good store by them .... The mirror of our mind reflects to us what we present to it; all which we purposely leave behind, that great hideous humpback of unknown, unthought-of, unenquired-for sin, grows, day by day, the more deformed, ... because, in our ignorance of it, we are continually aggravating it. (Pusey 9)

Philip's external perfection and self-righteousness reinforce each other, such that the only sins he has are those that derive from thinking he has none. He is insulated from an awareness of his sin by his "evil crust" of knowingness.

Guy, however, is patterned after the publican. He is quick to self-accusation and penitence for all his faults, both great (such as the desire for murderous revenge on Philip) and small (such as failing to enjoy himself when others are trying to give him pleasure). The visibility of his characteristic temptation – outbreaks of temper – prevents him from deceiving himself about his own perfection and thereby instills the habit of confession that prevents hidden sins from developing.[17] Guy's conscientious confessions of slight faults may seem overstrained, but Yonge's point is clearly that Guy's awareness of his sinful predilections keeps him in a salutary state of spiritual dependence on God and on other Christians.

Also unlike Philip, Guy is acutely conscious of a gap between the appearance and reality of one's moral state. His humility enables him to shrug off the praise of others, declaring, for example, that his dependents at Redclyffe "would be sure to praise me, if I was anything short of a brute" (27). When Mrs. Edmonstone praises his "victory" over his temper after one run-in with Philip, Guy replies, "The victory will be if the inward feeling as well as the outward token is ever subdued" (139). When Guy learns of Philip's inquiries about him with the tutors and tradesmen at Oxford, Guy "only wished his true character was as good as what would be reported of him" (274).

Guy's inner posture of penitence is reflected in the intuitive sympathy he always feels for other penitents. His grandfather's long years of repentance from his hasty words that caused Guy's parents' deaths have profoundly colored Guy's moral sentiments. When speaking of Charles I, whom all Yonge's "good" characters revere, Guy's comment is that "his heart was too tender, his repentance too deep for his friends to add one word even in jest to the heap of reproach" (64). The Innominato of *I Promessi Sposi* draws Guy's sympathy as well: "I never read anything equal to the repentance of the nameless man" (44).

This humility is replicated in Amy, even as Philip's hard self-confidence is echoed in Laura. When Guy treats Amy as morally superior to himself, Amy "exclaimed to herself how far from his equal she was – how weak, idle, and self-pleasing she felt herself to be" (139). After their engagement, Amy's biggest fear is that Guy "should take me for more than I am worth" (196).

For the large middle section of the novel, the moral contours of the paired opposites are sufficiently transparent to the reader. By the time Guy and Philip meet in Italy after Guy and Amy's wedding, the reactions of the two men to each other are perfectly predictable, and the reactions of the reader no less so. We hate Philip and love Guy with equal intensity. But just when we think we have mastered the novel's contrasting case studies, Yonge plots a second and more profound reversal. Philip insists on traveling through a fever-infested region of Italy; Guy decides that he and Amy, who is now pregnant, will take a different route. Philip attributes Guy's decision to stubborn pique, but when Philip falls ill of the fever, Guy and Amy come to nurse him. Philip recovers, though never completely, but Guy contracts the fever and dies.

In a series of painful scenes, Philip comes to realize not only that he has been unjust and even malicious to Guy, but also that his own small-mindedness and self-righteousness are the cause of Guy's death. Now it is Philip who "shrink[s] into himself" at praise (480), who engages in merciless "self-reproach" (543), and who embraces "the load and the stings of a profound repentance" (511). Philip's repentance is sharpened by the unstinting forgiveness Guy offers Philip, even before Philip manages to ask for it, and by Guy's total absence of reproach for any of Philip's misdeeds. Guy's saintliness was remarkable before, but this act of forgiveness is the most extravagant instance of it. Amy's ability to follow Guy's lead in forgiving the man whose malice resulted in her husband's death is a similarly extravagant gesture, showing how Guy's virtue engenders a small but durable climate of limit-experience around him.

Rather than ending the book with this closure, however, Yonge is far from finished. In the concluding section following Guy's death – almost a fifth of the novel's total length – Yonge reveals the secret she encoded in the title to the novel: that the central figure of the novel is not Guy but Philip. The "heir of Redclyffe" seems a romantic way of referring to Guy, who becomes the baronet on the death of his grandfather just as the novel's action opens. But as a number of critics have noted, this means that the heir apparent to Redclyffe for the majority of the novel is Philip. When he finally inherits Redclyffe after causing Guy's death, Philip asserts his position as the novel's title character; the reader realizes that Philip's inheritance is the *telos* that the title has suggested all along. The character the reader has been led to regard as the antagonist is suddenly reintroduced to the reader as the protagonist.

By the end of the novel the reader is asked to regard Philip as a paragon indeed: Charlie, who of all the characters is the most chary of praise and the most contrary to Philip, finally says, "I think him positively noble and grand, and when I see proofs of his being entirely repentant, I perceive he is a thorough great man" (586–87). In the novel's long afterglow, as the characters' acute grief over Guy fades, we see that Guy – a Christ figure – was sacrificed in order to redeem Philip and set him on a course to true greatness. Guy's saintliness, especially his final act of forgiveness, is the gesture of extravagance that redescribes human experience, and it makes possible Philip's transformation from arid self-righteousness to salvific and redemptive penitence.

Philip thus comes to resemble the most prominent Pharisee in Christian history: the apostle Paul.[18] Yonge's descriptions of Philip's dawning self-knowledge in Italy clearly show that she wants her readers to see Philip as an analogue of Paul. When Philip finally learns that Guy wanted his one thousand pounds in order to endow an Anglican sisterhood (and not to pay off gambling debts as Philip supposed), "Philip heard as if a flash of light was blinding him. ... Philip had sunk on his knees, ... in an agony of self-abasement before the goodness he had so relentlessly persecuted" (463). Later the narrator again describes Philip's growing self-awareness with a metaphor directly drawn from the biblical account of Paul's conversion: "[T]he scales of self-admiration fell from his eyes, and he knew both himself and his cousin" (469).[19] Saul/Paul's dramatic conversion from zealous (but half-taught) persecutor of the faithful to suffering missionary to the Gentiles is a fitting paradigm for Philip's radical redirection.

*****

Many if not most readers have resisted the shift in sympathy that the novel asks of them regarding Philip; yet I suggest that in this resistance can be traced the confrontational effect of the novel as a parable. Disbelief, or a denial of the realism of Philip's repentance, is one form of that resistance. An otherwise laudatory review in *The Christian Remembrancer* objected that "the depth and reality of Philip's repentance, considering his intense egotism and self-sufficient vanity, does not, we must confess, approve itself altogether to our belief" ("Miss Yonge's Novels" 63). When we remember that it is precisely in the intrusion of the extraordinary into otherwise ordinary or conventional realism that parables transmit their aggressively subversive message about ultimate reality, we can see that Philip's allegedly unbelievable repentance is the pivot for the whole book.

Even those who do not object to Philip's repentance on the grounds of probability may still be unwilling to grant the sympathy the novel claims for Philip in its final section. Antagonism to Philip formed the chief part of the criticism that was offered by Yonge's family and close friends when they read *Heir* in manuscript, according to Christabel Coleridge's authorized biography of Yonge. Sir John Coleridge desired that Amy's child would be male because "the public would never stand seeing Philip heir of Redclyffe" (Coleridge 166). Yonge's brother Julian wanted to horsewhip Philip around the quad at his Oxford college. A *Fraser's* reviewer in 1854 declared that Philip "never wins our cordial love and sympathy, even in the most bitter of his trials" ("*Heartsease*" 502).

As Robert Lee Wolff points out with more detachment, "Philip . . . is so disagreeable that the reader can easily emerge from the book without realizing that Charlotte Yonge intended Philip's development to be as important as Guy's" (134). This is at least as true of modern critics as of Victorian readers. Vineta Colby says the "long, tearful epilogue" is "[f]aulty . . . both emotionally and artistically" (201). Other critics, including Barbara Dennis, ignore the novel's final section, giving the impression that Philip's faults alone are worth comment.

Hence the ending is frequently regarded as an artistic problem – namely, that Yonge fails to win the reader's sympathy for the repentant Philip. In fact Yonge's master-stroke as a parabolist lies in this apparent failure: in the reader's resistance to Philip's transformation, the novel exposes the reader's own likeness to Philip. Readers who cannot believe in Philip's repentance align themselves with the earlier Pharisaical Philip, who refused to believe in the sincerity of Guy's repentance from his negligible faults of temper. Similarly, the readers who do not believe that Philip's change is realistic privilege their own "knowledge of mankind" over the power of God to save even self-righteous sinners (73). The reader is made to feel that her moral judgment of Philip is erroneous. For some readers, (mis)led early on to take Philip as "one of those perfect heroes whom nobody likes," it will in fact have been twice erroneous. The "real" outcome of Philip's life as Yonge narrates it thus requires skepticism towards conventional or "worldly" psychological expectations at the same time that it requires credence in a worldview structured by the gospels – a worldview that remains, in nineteenth-century Britain as in first-century Palestine, radically subversive of conventional moral ideas. *Heir* therefore fulfills the thesis of Caroline Levine that realist suspense narratives inculcate skepticism about what one thinks one knows.

At first Philip seemed close to the kingdom of God while Guy seemed distant; then Philip seemed remote while Guy received justification, as did the penitent sinner in the parable. But finally Philip, in his repentance, is shown to be closer to God than, perhaps, the readers in their self-complacent condemnation of Philip. Readers' reluctance to sympathize with the changed Philip points to their secret Pharisaical sense of moral superiority to him. In Pusey's words, they are guilty of "out-Pharisee-ing the Pharisee" in their very act of visiting righteous indignation on Philip. The novel's ability to induce skepticism towards the conventional morality of the characters, that is, to disrupt the readers' confidence in their judgment of the characters' proximity to the kingdom of God, is preparatory to the challenge to readers' self-righteousness.

The full interpretation of this perlocutionary novel therefore comes in the reader's imitative enactment of the repentance of Philip. Andrew Miller's observation on Newman's critique of complacent knowingness is apposite here: Newman's therapy for the moral and mental torpor induced by knowingness is "a particular interpretive practice – one that turns on our abilities to convert words through our response to them, thus allowing them to convert us – on which conversion our own salvation depends" (160). This is the mode in which parables operate: according to David Lyle Jeffrey, "It is the parable that interprets the sinner. . . . As a narrative of repentance, the purpose of such a parable [as the Pharisee and the publican] is evidently to initiate the possibility of repentance in a reader who is not yet irremediably hard-hearted" (361, 363). In other words, the parable speaks to those who are zealous but half-taught.

That the parabolic valences of *Heir* have not been noticed either by contemporaneous or modern critics actually strengthens my argument. We have already observed that Yonge was conscious, perhaps playfully so, of misleading certain of her readers who were not sufficiently attuned to the way her fictional technique serves the text's moral provocation. Yonge was fully aware that a good many of the novel's enthusiastic readers did not perceive her central moral message. Though pleased to read a positive review in *The Times*, she also wrote, "It seems to me *exactly the world's judgment* of Guy and Philip" (Romanes 69, emphasis added). The reviewer's complaint – that "[t]he lower orders in the moral world must feel themselves not so much encouraged or edified as crushed by the self-abasement of one so superior as Guy. His humility tramples us into the dust" – makes clear that the reviewer was not of the penitential disposition to receive the instruction the novel offers ("The Heir of Redclyffe" 9). From the standpoint of Tractarian morality discussed above, this reviewer, despite his geniality, shows a damnable disposition to be satisfied with remaining among the "lower orders in the moral world" in which he ironically places himself. Yonge's full consciousness of "the world's" erroneous judgment of her novel, even when that judgment is largely positive, implies that the novel's ability to provoke different levels of reaction and understanding from differently-disposed readers was part of the design of the novel.

Nevertheless, one would like to find some corroboration of this reading among the multifarious responses to the novel, and I am pleased to find it in the one reader who was probably most attuned to Yonge's aims. As Yonge's mother recorded in a letter to Dyson following one of the endless discussions about *Heir* among the circle of Yonge's family and neighbors, "Mr. Keble says everybody is like Philip" (Coleridge 189). This statement is more startling than it might first appear. There is ample evidence that the novel's many eager male readers, from army officers to undergraduates, widely identified with Guy, and it was Guy with whom the female readers fell in love (Battiscome 76). But Keble believed, as did Trench and Pusey no less than Yonge, that the path to being a saint lies through the painful recognition of oneself in the Pharisee: every morally conscientious person tends towards Pharisaism unless he or she, like Guy, practices continual repentance from minor failings, including the very complacency that arises from meticulous conformity with everyday morality. The novel's extraordinary achievement lies in its ability, whether latent or realized, to reproduce this shock of recognition in the reader. Just when the reader is ready to horsewhip Philip, the reader is told – like David was told by Nathan – "Thou art the man." As Philip's story shows, only when one's hidden sin is exposed does the repentance, which can eventually produce the saintly purity of a Guy Morville, occur. The novel instigates this process in the reader via the character of Philip while also making its results imminently attractive via the character of Guy.

Reading *The Heir of Redclyffe* as a Victorian retelling of the parable of the Pharisee and the publican contextualizes the tension between Yonge's realism and didacticism while also explaining Yonge's willingness to provoke the disbelief and hostility of her readers in the novel's much-maligned ending. Yonge not only retells the parable in modern dress, but she also recreates its subversive effect by her double reversal that challenges the reader's presumptive moral certainties and potentially incites repentance.

# 4
# Prodigal Sons in the Fiction of Margaret Oliphant

The prodigal son was a trope Oliphant returned to again and again throughout her long career as a writer. From the sustained subtext of *The Perpetual Curate* (1864) to the recurring subject of the late novels *The Prodigals and Their Inheritance* (1885) and *Who Was Lost and Is Found* (1894), as well as the short stories "The Open Door" (1882) and "The Land of Suspense" (1897), Oliphant used the parable in her fiction to think through moral, relational, and existential dilemmas. In a number of ways this parable is particularly apropos for her use. Its focus on a domestic conflict is in line with her favorite subject matter, and its incidents intersected with her own life in poignant ways. Oliphant's two surviving sons were perennial disappointments, remaining dependent on their mother until their deaths in their mid-thirties. Not for nothing did Oliphant write in her *Autobiography* of her attachment to her late husband's painting "The Prodigal" – one of the few that remained to her – calling it "a very touching picture" (*Autobiography* 62).

All of the fiction Oliphant wrote on this theme is conspicuously autobiographical. In *The Perpetual Curate*, her playful treatment of prodigality shades at moments into serious thought about the existential questions posed by the parable, in which the painful notes of Oliphant's grief at her daughter's recent death can be clearly heard. In the late work, the prodigal sons – and especially their relationships with their mothers – closely resemble Oliphant's own struggles with her adult sons.[1] It is notable that her prodigals always appear in pairs: the son and his friend of *Who Was Lost and*

*Is Found*, the two exiled brothers of *The Prodigals*, and even Tom Wodehouse and Jack Wentworth of *The Perpetual Curate*, written while her own sons were young boys. Writing of her son Cyril on the day of his death, she directly borrowed the idiom of the parable as she prayed for God's mercy on him: "He has sinned, he has sinned, and done evil in thy sight" (*Autobiography* 44).

Hence the simplicity of the parable was well suited for Oliphant's portrayals of troubled filial relationships. Yet it is also true that the complexity of the parable – particularly its counterintuitive refusal of the apparent justice of the older brother's claims – opened opportunities for her to explore a question that she struggled with all her life, namely, the inequality of human suffering. As old as Job and as new as each day's headlines, this problem appears in various forms throughout Oliphant's oeuvre, from her first nonfiction book, *Sundays* (1858), to her 1895 *Blackwood's* article "Fancies of a Believer."

This chapter will first establish a nuanced picture of Oliphant's religious views as they relate to and are made visible in some of her various uses of the parable of the prodigal son. Following this, I will closely examine Oliphant's use of the parable of the prodigal son as a subtext to *The Perpetual Curate* as she playfully deconstructs the parable's conventional application yet also registers her deepening tensive response to the teachings and mysteries contained in it. Ultimately, this analysis of Oliphant's use of the parable not only demonstrates the seriousness with which Oliphant faced personal theological questions, but also the sophistication of her handling of the parable genre in its capacity to disorient in order to reorient. Oliphant does not ground her entire oeuvre in a particular and articulated religious worldview, as Yonge does, but she does use her fiction to probe religious or metaphysical questions.

The prodigal-son subtext in *The Perpetual Curate* works in at least two related but distinct ways. First, the parable provides a basic plot structure that Oliphant plays with in the novel, turning the familiar plot around, experimenting with alternative outcomes, and offering deflating, unsentimentalized reinterpretations. This project is in keeping with Oliphant's usual register of social comedy. As an aspect of this narratorial engagement with the parable, we will also see that the parable provides a recognizable structure for the characters in the novel, whose expectations and responses to their situations are conditioned by the parable. The comically deflating revision of the parable Oliphant offers is sometimes tied to the inappropriateness of the characters' casting themselves and others in roles drawn from the parable.

Second, and perhaps counterintuitively given my previous point, the parable offers Oliphant a framework for the examination of serious theological and existential questions, especially regarding providential justice. Oliphant was writing *The Perpetual Curate* at the time of the death of her ten-year-old daughter Maggie in Rome. The existential struggle captured in Oliphant's account of her grief, later published in her *Autobiography*, emphasizes her sense of the injustice of her suffering. It has been assumed that this event leaves no significant mark on the novel, which "resumed in May [1864], with no noticeable drop in the tempo of the comedy" after only a one-month suspension following Maggie's death (Shattock, "Making of a Novelist" 118). However, the same *cri de coeur* about providential justice also surfaces repeatedly in the novel: in the assorted predicaments that force Frank to suffer the calumny deserved by others, in Frank's defense of Protestantism to Gerald, and especially in its sustained engagement with the parable of the prodigal son.[2] When we attend to what Oliphant is doing in such moments, it becomes clear why Oliphant would write to John Blackwood that the novel was "the sharer of my inmost thoughts" (Oliphant and Coghill 191).

It may seem to many readers that the comic deflation of the parable is incompatible with the parable being an occasion for serious theological reflection. In other words, it would be easy to assume that Oliphant's playful irreverence towards the story would indicate uninterest in or even hostility towards the parable's theological content. But this assumption, I argue, would be a mistake, both by reason of the nature of the parable genre and by reason of Oliphant's particular religious disposition. As we will see, Oliphant's unorthodox deconstructions of the parable veer back around towards orthodoxy, and the conclusion of *The Perpetual Curate* seems to underscore a belief in the trustworthiness of divine justice despite abundant evidence to the contrary.

Moreover, as we have already explored, parables live in the tension between the iconic and the iconoclastic. It is equally mistaken to strip the parables of their artistry and playfulness, as Jülicher and his followers did, or to strip them of their theology, as Crossan did in emphasizing their playfulness. In this light, Oliphant's treatment of the parable seems to anticipate later developments in parable theory which remained unavailable to the professional theological establishment of her day. Oliphant's take is refreshing compared with the deadly seriousness of both traditional Christian defenders of the Bible and unorthodox or freethinking critics of the Bible, all of whom turned the parable of the prodigal son into a sticky-sweet celebration of the Victorian cult of domesticity. Oliphant's treatment is bracingly, even abrasively, challenging to those conventional Victorian pieties and yet ultimately affirmative of the fatherhood of God. That Oliphant would make a parable the compass in her lifelong effort to navigate her own faith and doubt in God's justice is seen, in this light, to express a profound theological intuition. Since parables by their nature are suggestive rather than determinative, it is entirely fitting that Oliphant makes a parable central to her engagement of Christian mysteries, and that her use of the parable employs the characteristic parabolic element of reversal in the destabilization of moral and theological platitudes.

\* \* \* \* \*

Oliphant's description of her late article "Fancies of a Believer" (1895) – that it is "not what is called orthodox, nor is it unorthodox"– could equally well describe her religious disposition generally (Oliphant and Coghill 415). She opens the article by asserting that her belief in the core doctrines of Christianity is unambivalent. Yet she proceeds to speculate about theological questions, particularly those of theodicy and the efficacy of prayer, which are not "made clear by revelation" and in which the believer therefore "may be permitted to do his best to explain to himself" ("Fancies" 237). In fact, her stated purpose in the article is "to let loose the more fanciful and even fantastic impulses of the mind in subordination to a humble Christian fidelity to the faith of the Gospel" (237). Clearly she thinks that speculation within certain bounds does not threaten fidelity, and a careful reading of even some of Oliphant's many journalistic and autobiographical comments about religion makes clear that both bedrock conviction and forthright protest are ineluctable elements of her religious life.

I will show in a moment that this insight has largely eluded critical responses to Oliphant, which have recently tended to focus on her anti-idealism and suspicion to the exclusion of her idealism and conviction. But first I will point briefly to two late texts as illustrations of Oliphant's troubled fidelity: *Who Was Lost and Is Found* and "The Open Door," both of which engage the parable of the prodigal son. In these texts, as in her autobiographical uses of the same parable, Oliphant's trust in divine justice bumps up against her raw experience to produce a painful tension.

In *Who Was Lost and Is Found*, Oliphant alludes directly to the parable not only in the title but also at several points in the novel. The aging mother Mrs. Oglivy is constantly on the watch for the return of her ne'er-do-well son Robbie. She frequently imagines the moment of his return and explicitly compares herself to the father watching down the road for the returning prodigal. But Robbie's actual return is nothing like her pious fantasies. He comes at the one moment in years when she is not hoping to see him, and she does not even recognize him at first:

> She had looked for it so long, for years and years and years, anticipated every particular of it: how she would recognize him afar off, and go out to meet him, like the father of the prodigal . . . how he would come to her all in a moment, and fling himself down by her side, with his head in her lap, as had been one of his old ways. . . . But never like this. (67)

Robbie's manner is sullen and morose, he complains about the lack of spirits in the house, and he rebukes his mother for her delayed recognition. As the book goes on, he deceives his mother about his criminal record, tries to extort money from her, and forces her and her household to cater to a wide variety of unreasonable whims, all the while behaving with unpardonable rudeness.[3] Mrs. Oglivy repeatedly struggles to come to terms with the disappointment of Robbie's return, again comparing herself to the father of the parable:

> Perhaps in his heart the father of the prodigal learned this lesson too, and knew that, even with the best robe upon him, and the ring on his finger and the shoes on his feet, he was still hankering after the husks which the swine eat, and their company (337–38).[4]

Oliphant's reinscription of the parable in this novel, then, is largely deflating. Not only does the nineteenth-century version of the story include a number of unsavory possibilities that run against the grain of the parable, but the narrator even reads those possibilities back into the original story. In fact Oliphant's take on the parable in this novel is in keeping with her tendency, examined by Margarete Rubik in reference to other novels, to subvert conventional Victorian myths of filial piety.[5] Certainly Oliphant is far from being like those, as she put it, "to whom religion is but a system of mild and sentimental prettiness."[6]

Ultimately, however, Mrs. Oglivy's "tolerant, all-explaining, all-pardoning love" is both ridiculed and valorized (370). Her pitiful willingness to sacrifice every desire, comfort, and shred of dignity for her ungrateful son's sake is given a heroic cast when she actually comes between her son and a bullet from his accomplice's gun. This action finally awakens Robbie's tenderness for his mother, and he settles down into idle but respectable domestic life by marrying his childhood sweetheart. The narrator concedes that there was no "great moral improvement in Robbie," but it is enough to make the family happy: "a little went a long way with those two women, who loved him" (370).

In "The Open Door" (1882), a stronger and more positive connection is made between the parent's undying love of the wayward child and God's eternal welcome. In this supernatural short story, a wailing spirit haunts the empty door frame of a ruined outbuilding. The open door of the title refers not just to the empty door frame but more pointedly to the eternal opportunity for the spirit to return to heaven. The spirit is finally exorcised by an experienced, kindly priest who recognizes the spirit as an erring son who, long ago, returned to his mother's door the day after her death. Calling the young man by name, Dr. Montcrieff cries,

> Do you think [your mother] would ever close her door on her own lad? Do ye think the Lord would ever close the door, ye faint-hearted creature? No! ... And her too, poor woman! ... Her you are calling on. She's no here. You'll find her with the Lord. Go there and seek her, not here. Do you hear me, lad? Go after her there. He'll let you in, though it's late. (205)

When the rector prays to God to "Let that woman there draw him inower!" the spirit seems finally to rush in the empty door frame it has been haunting and is not heard again. The rector's speech and the tale's outcome valorize the link between the mother's unfailing love for her wayward son and God's eternal welcome to the penitent, even after death. This sentiment is a close echo of Oliphant's own reflection after the death of her son Cyril:

> O my, my father almighty, I am not afraid of thee. Thou wilt cradle him in thy arms. Thou wilt comfort him as one whom his mother comforteth. He has sinned, he has sinned, and done evil in thy sight. . . . Lord of Lords thou art holding him awful in thy arms before he begins the sweet, the better life. (*Autobiography* 44)

In this passage, Oliphant paraphrases the confession of the prodigal son ("Father, I have sinned against heaven, and done what is evil in thy sight" [Luke 15:18]) by way of expressing her certainty that God ("O my, my father") cannot but be more merciful than is a mother towards the failings of her child.

Clearly, then, our understanding of Oliphant must make room for a deep current of affectively-charged Christian faith as well as for her brisk debunking of religious and domestic sentimentality. At the same time, we should not conclude that Oliphant was simply an unreflecting believer, finding vapid and sentimental consolation when and where she needed it while remaining scathingly clear-sighted about life in general. Such a view does not do justice to the pertinacity with which she struggled through her considered theological stances, nor to the depth of her theological reading.[7] Oliphant was reflective and self-conscious about everything, and her religious beliefs are no exception. She was not able to seal off her religious beliefs from her lived experience, drawing on religion for consolation in dark moments while remaining oblivious to the implications of the truth claims of Christianity. For example, she frequently wondered how to reconcile the biblical promises that prayers offered in faith will be answered with the fact that her own prayers for her sons were not answered.[8]

In particular, the theological question that drew her consideration and frustration again and again was the problem of providential justice. If the world is ruled by a just God, why do the innocent often suffer and the guilty often thrive? Expressions of this problem appear in many of the personal passages in the *Autobiography*, particularly in the passages in which she reacts to her bereavements. In the early stages of Oliphant's agonizing grief over the loss of her daughter Maggie, she complains of the unfairness of God in taking her daughter while other people's children are not touched:

> I am neither better nor worse than my brother Frank who has never known a trouble in his family – I am neither better nor worse than my dear friend who is so much happier, so much more blessed than I, but I am smitten and they are spared – why is it? ... I have not shrunk from any of my duties – I have faced the burden and borne it and never tried to put off any part of it upon the shoulders of others – God help me – does that make me think that I had a right to demand from him that divine cordial of happiness which I have been enjoying for these years past, but which now he has deprived me of? (10)

By putting this question to herself she both expresses her sense of defiance – her desire to demand that God answer to her for the justice of his actions – and accuses herself of unreasonableness or audacity in doing so.[9] Notwithstanding the intense personal register of this writing, Oliphant handles her grief with the tools that are habitual to her as a novelist; here she uses her signature technique of seamlessly presenting a character both as she appears to herself and as she appears to others. Oliphant's outrage at God's apparent injustice is thus laid alongside her consciousness of the absurdity of her expectation that justice be done in a way conformable to her views. Oliphant concludes, "His dealings are unequal beyond all doubt or question – I can trust Him through all my doubts that somehow it is right, but I cannot shut my eyes to this strange inequality" (12). The consciousness of "this strange inequality" persists in her religious thought throughout her life. In 1895 after her sons' deaths, Oliphant described "the *continual appeal I am always making to heaven and earth, consciously or unconsciously*, saying often, I know, as I have no right to say, 'Is this fair, – is it right that I should be so bowed down to the earth and everything taken from me?'" (*Autobiography* 99, emphasis added). Similarly, in "Fancies of a Believer," she concisely expresses her abiding faith alongside her resistance to platitudes: "It is sometimes a little relief to escape from the conventional bonds of resignation and submission and say, without any failure of trust or confidence that He knows best, that He has been cruel" (252–53).

In making this more or less constant protest against the "unequal" dealings of God, Oliphant seems to chime with the outrage of the older brother in the parable of the prodigal son, who complains that his virtue does not bring its just reward. When Oliphant writes, "I have not shrunk from any of my duties . . . does that make me think that I had a right to demand from him that divine cordial of happiness. . . ?" she sounds rather like the older son telling his father, "These many years do I serve thee, neither transgressed I at any time thy commandment: and yet thou never gavest me a kid, that I might make merry with my friends" (Luke 15:29). The parable of the prodigal son is not typically read as being about providential justice, but it is clear from the way Oliphant used the parable in *The Perpetual Curate* that she considered the parable in that light. Whereas in her later fiction, after her sons' failures had become evident, Oliphant used the parable to register her hopes and frustrations about her sons, in *The Perpetual Curate*, written partly after Maggie's death, the parable serves her to confront her struggle with the apparent injustice of God.

*****

Religious themes such as I have been exploring appear very little in critical work on Oliphant.[10] The recent surge of interest in Oliphant, driven largely by feminist recovery efforts, has emphasized works such as *Miss Marjoribanks* (1866) and *Phoebe Junior* (1876) in which cherished Victorian ideals are noticeably upended. In both *Miss Marjoribanks* and *Phoebe Junior*, the capable, pragmatic heroines choose to marry men they do not love with the intention of guiding their unimpressive husbands into creditable political careers.[11] Critics whose primary interest is in Oliphant's treatment of gender politics have preferred to talk about these novels or others, such as *Kirsteen* (1890) and *Hester* (1883), that feature independent women and men who are usually weak, vain, petty, or insipid.[12] Oliphant's domestic comedies in general amply affirm the arguments of scholars who have emphasized that realism is not merely ideologically and epistemologically reassuring.

*The Perpetual Curate*, however, is more conventional formally and ideologically than those more widely-discussed books. It ends with the presumed marriage of the well-matched hero and heroine, who are thoroughly in love and worthy of each other. Oliphant's characteristic deflation of conjugal ideals is displaced from the main characters to secondary characters, such as Mr. and Mrs. Morgan, who begin their mature married life with expectations of long-delayed but unmitigated bliss, only to discover each other's petty vanities and foibles. Frank Wentworth and Lucy Wodehouse, however, are thoroughly genteel, consistently high-minded, and capable workers in their spheres. That is not to say, of course, that they are perfect or untouched by irony, but their mostly endearing faults arise from an excess of high principles rather than a deficiency, and their consciousness of their own follies usually keeps them from being priggish.

This conventionality seems to account for the book's popularity with its first audience, as Joanne Shattock observes: "It was the very ordinariness of the story, the quietness, even dullness of the life described and yet made interesting, which the reviewers emphasized" ("Making of a Novelist" 120). Oliphant herself seems to have been almost embarrassed by the book's rosy ending, forestalling criticism of it by having Frank's caustic Aunt Leonora berate his "vulgarity" in "com[ing] to an ending like a trashy novel" (535). Critics seem to agree more or less with Leonora that the novel's neat ending is "weak folly and nonsense that no sensible man would have anything to say to" (535); at any rate they have had relatively little to say about *The Perpetual Curate*, which has received little sustained attention.[13]

But *The Perpetual Curate* is a more complicated book than has been recognized, and the parable of the prodigal son is a key subtext in it. Two minor characters, Frank's oldest brother Jack Wentworth and Lucy's older brother Tom Wodehouse, are repeatedly referred to as prodigal sons. Both of them are estranged from their fathers and are profligate wasters of their patrimony. Oliphant's use of the parable, though richly comical, is not merely facetious: she substantively wrestles with the dilemmas the parable presents for a person of faith, as Frank is conscious of finding himself in the role of the prodigal's (self-)righteous brother, and late in the novel he resolves upon a course of prodigality as well. Throughout, Oliphant struggles with the parable's apparent injustice—the returned prodigal is received with honor that is not accorded to the inoffensive older brother, yet the older brother is rebuked for objecting to this.

As I noted, Oliphant's investment in this theological problem has largely been neglected by critics. Oliphant's obvious interest and strength in writing social comedy has effectively held off critical study of the ways that her religious thought surfaced in her fiction. Moreover, her penchant for characters and scenarios that defy literary and ideological conventions has facilitated a focus on Oliphant's anti-idealism.[14] Margarete Rubik writes that "Margaret Oliphant's answers to moral questions often subvert the high-flown Victorian code of behavior, which she regards as unrealistic, over exacting, or even hypocritical. It is typical of Oliphant to debunk grandiose poses and lofty pretenses and to view characters from a prosaic, unidealized angle" ("Subversion" 63). More specifically, as regards the literary convention of poetic justice, "The belief in such a cozy scheme of timely punishments and rewards seems to her childish and naïve" ("Subversion" 59).[15] Similarly, Merryn Williams writes that in Oliphant's fiction, "We are forced to re-examine the 'modern sentimental ethic' that goodness brings its own reward" (*Margaret Oliphant* 75).[16] Such generalizations are partly true, yet they fail to capture the complexity of Oliphant, who not only remained a professing Christian all her life but also wrote with subtlety and sophistication about theological figures and controversies in a number of essays in *Blackwood's Edinburgh Magazine.* Joseph O'Mealy has pointed to the presence of idealist tendencies in Oliphant's comic fiction, observing that Oliphant's clerical characters "have a pastoral side as priests and ministers, and we are given a sense of their spiritual struggles, hopes, and fears, as well as being permitted to witness their activities as intermediaries between God and man" ("Scenes" 254–5). In particular, Frank's "keen competitive instincts in questions of territoriality and power are undeniable, but the other side of Frank Wentworth, his genuine commitment to a priesthood of service and spiritual aid, should not be overlooked" (257). However, O'Mealy's conclusions are merely antiquarian, demonstrating only that Oliphant accurately rendered the tone of clerical vocations in the mid-Victorian era.[17]

In this chapter, I pursue O'Mealy's consideration of the idealism that coexists with anti-idealism in *The Perpetual Curate*. The social comedy of *The Perpetual Curate* need not exclude serious metaphysical questioning, any more than the social comedy of *Miss Marjoribanks* excludes serious, if ambivalent, treatment of feminine ideology.[18] It can be difficult to trace the presence of such questions in the comic fiction, because they are always in danger of being laughed aside by the irony directed against the characters by the narrator, by the other characters, and not infrequently by themselves.[19] The high-minded ideals and theological convictions of the characters are noticeably and comically susceptible to social pressure, or to personal vanity or desire. Yet *The Perpetual Curate* engages theological questions that buzz in the background, so to speak, breaking into the foreground occasionally so as to generate a tension between the dominant anti-idealist note of the comedy and the desperately serious voice we hear in parts of the *Autobiography*. Moreover, the tension seen in Oliphant "between traditionalism and subversion, between adhering to conventional values and radically challenging Victorian ideals" is congruent with the nature of parables, as we have seen (Rubik, *Novels* 2–3).

*The Perpetual Curate* is colored by a tension between an idealized notion of providential justice and a disillusioned acceptance of its absence, and it is colored as well by the self-awareness with which Oliphant confronted that tension. Elisabeth Jay suggests that "Oliphant's desire to be true to her perception of life's apparent plotlessness led her to push against the limiting structures provided by providential explanations." In the novels, this disposition "led to a marked repudiation of that favourite Victorian device, the final chapter in which order and happiness are reimposed" ("Introduction" xiv).[20] If Jay is right about the close connection between Oliphant's own weakened sense of providence and the ambivalent endings of her novels, then *The Perpetual Curate* is an important countervailing text.[21] In its unusually settled and optimistic ending, the novel suggests Oliphant's hard-won affirmation of belief in providence, in which she persists despite the mystery with which it is shrouded. When this belief was most severely tested in her life is exactly when it most strongly emerged in her fiction.

\* \* \* \* \*

Oliphant's confrontation with the question of providential justice dovetails effectively with her use of the prodigal son parable as a subtext to *The Perpetual Curate*, centering on Tom Wodehouse and Jack Wentworth. Tom left home in disgrace seventeen years before, and his much younger half-sister Lucy does not even know of his existence. He has returned to hide in Carlingford, hoping to avoid arrest and prosecution in London, where he has been discovered forging his father's signature on bills. Forging his father's signature is a close nineteenth-century equivalent to spending his patrimony before his father's death. His return to his father is therefore deeply troubled. Not only is Tom in no way repentant – he frequently avers that the signature he used was, after all, his own name – but he only emerges from hiding on his father's death, surprising everyone, including his sisters, by taking the son's place in his father's funeral procession. His return is entirely mercenary: he is eager to get his hands on his dying father's property and has no interest in reconciliation with his father. This family drama impinges on Frank's story when Tom's full sister, Mary Wodehouse, begs Frank to accept Tom as an incognito guest for the sake of his friendship with the Wodehouse family.

Jack Wentworth, for his part, has also been parted from his family for many years, running up debts that his father, with a half-dozen sons on his hands, is hard-pressed to pay and despairs of seeing an end to. Mr. Wentworth's disappointment with Jack surfaces in virtually every scene in which the squire appears. The squire's principal worry is that his many younger children, several of whom Jack has never seen, will be homeless and penniless when Jack inherits on Mr. Wentworth's death. Mr. Wentworth's yearning for his son – and its corollary in the bitterness he experiences with every fresh evidence of Jack's worthlessness – is palpable and touching. A telegram from Jack to Frank, received in Mr. Wentworth's presence, brings on the squire a "fit" of terror that Jack is corrupting Frank too. Like Tom, Jack also intrudes on Frank's home, coming to monitor the potentially loose lips of his vastly inferior accomplice and tool, Tom Wodehouse. He soon takes up residence with his aunts in the pose of a penitent, bent on turning from his evil and worldly ways, and they eagerly pounce upon him as a project of reformation.

Thus the "elegant prodigal" Jack and the "unlucky prodigal" Tom both enact highly problematic returns to their families, and both cause serious difficulties for Frank (203, 206). Frank, for his part, has had an unexceptional career as a clergyman up to the time his aunts come to Carlingford to investigate his fitness for the family living. Firm in her Evangelical principles, Leonora intends to deny Frank the living he has always expected if, as is the case, Frank is unyielding in his Ritualist persuasion. However, Frank's zeal in some extra-parochial missionary work among the poor of Wharfside causes Leonora to waver in her refusal, even as she enjoys the satisfaction of "reforming" Jack.

Not only does Oliphant resist the conventionally sentimental story of the repentant son and forgiving father, but she also twists the parable's use of the older brother by pointedly casting Frank in that role. Then, in a sustained, though sometimes ironic, discussion of providential justice, she invites the reader to sympathize with Frank's "natural" objections to the generous reception of Jack in the role of the returned prodigal.

When Frank visits his aunts on the first morning after Jack's arrival,

> Aunt Dora was ready to have sacrificed all the veal in the country in honour of Jack's repentance; and the Curate stood outside upon the threshold, looking at the scene with the strangest half-angry, half-comical realisation of the state of mind of the elder brother in the parable. He had himself been rather found fault with, excused, and tolerated, among his relations, but Jack had at once become master of the position, and taken possession of all their sympathies. Mr. Wentworth stood gazing at them, half-amused, and yet more angry than amused – feeling, with a little indignation, as was natural, that the pretended penitence of the clever sinner was far more effective and interesting than his own spotless loyalty and truth. (226)

Dora, the simple-minded but affectionate one of the aunts, artlessly rebukes Frank's incredulity with the very same biblical allusion that had occurred to him: "Oh, Frank ... isn't there joy in heaven over one sinner that repenteth? You're not going to be the wicked elder brother that grudged the prodigal his welcome – you're not going to give way to jealousy, Frank?" (228). Dora, Frank, and Jack all immediately understand the situation in light of the parable and readily "cast" Frank and Jack in the roles of the older and prodigal sons, respectively. However, in Oliphant's version, Frank comes out much better than the older brother of the parable whom he resembles. For one thing, the fact that Jack is only pretending to be repentant justifies Frank's refusal to join the celebration; and for another, Frank's consciousness of the ludicrousness of his position keeps him from being as offensively self-satisfied as the older brother of the parable. A little later Frank "began to realise, in a humorous way, his own sensations as he stood at the drawing-room door and recognized the prodigal on the sofa" (233). Nevertheless, the narrator suggests that Frank's indignation is "natural" and evidently expects the reader to agree.

Oliphant's revision of the parable is quite radical. This parable was very extensively treated by commentators and preachers during the period, but their interpretations are noticeably uncontroversial.[22] That the prodigal son story encapsulates "the gospel in a parable" was a commonplace of preachers. Every Victorian sermon and commentary on this parable I have seen emphasizes the repentance of the prodigal and the sinfulness of the older son.[23] Though most do not go as far as the Glasgow preacher Fergus Ferguson, who confidently claims that "The prodigal's fully amended behaviour followed his acceptance by his father," all assume that the prodigal's contrition is heartfelt and his repentance complete (143–44). Charles Spurgeon asserts that the prodigal "reformed from that very moment" of deciding to return to his father (69). Similarly, all emphasize the older brother's envy, arrogance, presumption, bitterness, disrespect to his father, and parsimoniousness. None concedes the least possibility that the older brother has a valid complaint against his father, however ungraciously expressed. This view, and the fact that it seems to have been a universal Victorian view, blunts some of the force of the parable, allowing the reader to dwell on the sentimentality of the story of reconciliation and to perpetuate the self-righteousness of the older brother. The familiarized Victorian interpretation elides the fact that, as Bernard Harrison points out, in this parable "the father's behaviour makes nonsense of common considerations of fairness and justice in the management of family affairs" (233).

Jesus's parable certainly does condemn the attitude of the older brother, who is as lost as the younger one only without the saving grace of knowing it. The whole triptych of parables which it concludes (the lost sheep, the lost coin, and the lost son) is told in response to the Pharisees who, observing Jesus's association with disreputable people, were heard muttering, "This man receiveth sinners, and eateth with them" (Luke 15:2). In an important sense, then, this second half of the parable is the climax of the series of parables, which, in portraying the mercy of God, simultaneously rebukes the disapproving sanctimoniousness that Luke attributes to the Pharisees. However, to rush to a moralizing condemnation of the older brother without acknowledging the justice of his claim actually reproduces his fundamental mistake – such moralizing effectively isolates the older brother (the Pharisees) as a "sinner," unlike the rest of us "good" people who have repented and come home to the father. Like the parable of the Pharisee and the publican, this parable loses its shock value when one's familiarity with orthodox interpretation predetermines one to identify with the prodigal (or a valorized version of him as the hero of the story who has repented and come home) and shun the Pharisaical older brother.

The power of Oliphant's reinscription, then, lies in the fact that she challenges that too-easy habit of identifying with the prodigal and pouring reproach on the older brother. The prodigals of *The Perpetual Curate*, like virtually all the prodigals in her fiction, are unlovely, unsentimentalized men, returning home only to further exploit the financial resources of their parents. This depiction makes visible a gap in the parable, which does not give any information about the state of the prodigal's soul or his conduct after his return. It is possible to read the prodigal's decision to return as purely mercenary, not humbly contrite. Moreover, Oliphant presents the older brother favorably, as having a valid cause for complaint in the injustice of the enthusiastic reception of the prodigal compared to the cool reception he has received.

These subversions could suggest that Oliphant is simply rejecting the message of the parable in favor of her unenthusiastic anti-idealism. Bringing the sublime story within mundane bounds shows not only its absurdity, but also its unreliability as a guide for human relationships. The ease with which the aunts are deceived implies that the plot the parable conditions people to expect is likely to mislead them in their ordinary life situations. Piously expecting the parable's plot to be effected in reality makes one culpably gullible in the hands of worldly and unscrupulous manipulators.

However, for several reasons I do not think that this temptingly simple conclusion is correct. Rather, I suggest that Oliphant's revision of the parable of the prodigal son actually strengthens and sharpens the parable by defamiliarizing it. One late twentieth-century exegete has said, "For the parable to be open-ended ... people almost need 'permission' to identify with the less attractive characters in the parable, to grumble with the vineyard workers or feel the chagrin of the elder brother, and thereby open themselves to the message of judgment or forgiveness" (Donahue 19). Oliphant's retelling of the parable in a manner favorable to the older brother effectively offers the reader that permission, and as we will see,

Frank does so as well in a sermon he preaches on the subject. Oliphant is not, of course, writing an exegesis of the parable. However, her altered retelling carries with it implicit interpretative claims. Inviting identification with the older brother makes visible the gap between ordinary moral relations, expressed by the older brother, and the claims of the gospel, expressed in the father's extravagance. According to Bernard Harrison, the parable's jolt appears precisely in the "gulf between the father's joy and the reaction of the elder son at being seriously asked to treat his wastrel brother as ... an object of immense intrinsic value" (234). Those who think they have understood the parable, but who have not found themselves in Frank's position testing its claims against their very different experience and feeling, have not really grasped the parable's counterintuitive message. The joyous reception of the prodigal and the summary condemnation of the older brother are merely platitudinous until one finds oneself in the position of Frank: unjustly neglected in favor of an undeserving rival.

Frank, then, *is* in such a position, and a great deal is at stake in how he responds. Can he believe in God's eternal welcome of the sinner, even when that sinner is as exasperating as Jack or Tom? Can he continue to believe in providential justice in the face of this evidence of what Oliphant elsewhere called the "strange inequality" of God's dealings? The ordeal Oliphant puts him through tests him on these points, and he expresses sentiments very similar to hers in the *Autobiography*. Like Oliphant, Frank wonders bitterly about "the contrarieties of the world": "how one man had to bear another's burdens ... , and how another man triumphed and came to success by means of the misfortunes of his friends. It was hard to tell how humankind got divided into these two great classes" of sufferers and beneficiaries (222). The outcome of Frank's cogitations, seen in his subsequent sermon and his conversation with Gerald, affirms Frank's relatively undramatic but continued faithfulness to the teachings of the parable.

*****

Having set up the confrontation between Frank and Jack in terms of the two sons of the parable, Oliphant extends the scenario of the parable into a direct consideration of the problem of providential justice. Frank's sense of injured merit intensifies as Frank is blamed for the seduction of a girl when Tom is the real culprit; later that day he attends at Mr. Wodehouse's deathbed where he exasperates and disappoints Lucy by talking to Mr. Wodehouse about his lack of a will. (Because she does not know that she has a brother, Lucy does not guess the danger that nothing at all will be left to her and Mary.) In between these momentous events Frank tries to write his sermon for the following morning, which, in his present state of revolt against the injustice of his situation, he plans as a defense of "that virtuous uninteresting elder brother [who is] not generally approved of" (233). His text is not propitious: "When the wicked man turneth away from the evil of his ways" (Ezekiel 18:27). Considering it, Frank

> began to wonder bitterly whether that ever happened, or if it was any good trying to bring it about. If it were really the case that Wodehouse, whom he had been labouring to save from the consequences of one crime, had, at the very crisis of his fate, perpetrated another of the basest kind, what was the good of wasting strength in behalf of a wretch so abandoned? Why should such a man be permitted to live to bring shame and misery on everybody connected with him? and why, when noxious vermin of every other description were hunted down and exterminated, should the vile human creature be spared to suck the blood of his friends? (248)

These un-priest-like thoughts echo the reflections of the day before, when Frank, both amused and angry, inwardly protested the injustice of his aunts' favor being given to Jack and withheld from himself, as well as of the day before that, when Frank wondered why some people thrive at others' cost. The passage in Ezekiel from which his sermon text is taken stresses that each person will receive the just reward or penalty of his own sin – a son departing from the righteous ways of his father will be punished, while a son departing from the wicked ways of his father will be preserved. This assertion of the reliability of divine justice enacted in individual cases troubles Frank in his palpable experience otherwise. He knows that he is expected to deliver a set of reassuring platitudes on providential justice, but in his present state of mind he cannot do so: Frank was "sore and wounded in his heart to feel how his own toils and honest purposes availed him nothing, and how all the interest and sympathy of bystanders went to the pretender. These sentiments naturally ... made composition difficult" (293). Like Oliphant herself in the *Autobiography*, Frank's thinking about Christian truth claims does not remain abstract; he must encounter the truth claim with reference to his concrete – and contrary – experience.

Indeed, throughout the day, Frank "saw nothing but misery, let him turn where he would – nothing but disgrace, misapprehension, unjust blame" (249). His effort to save Lucy from being left at Tom's mercy on her father's death is mistaken by his beloved for base mercenary calculation on his own part. Then, while the town readily believes Elsworthy's accusation against him, Frank cannot expose Tom's presumed guilt because of his delicate position vis-à-vis the just-bereaved Wodehouse family. Late at night when forced to complete the sermon, he bitterly reflects that providential justice is no more reliable than human justice: "It appeared to him, on the whole, that the wicked man was in every way the best off in this world, besides being wooed and besought to accept the blessings of the other" (293). The latter conclusion apparently arises from his thinking about the parable, in which the sinner is besought to accept the blessing of the father representing God, while the "virtuous uninteresting elder brother" is clearly censured. (If Frank were less bitter, he might have reflected that the older brother is also besought to accept the blessing of the father in that the father pleads with him to abandon his resentment and join the festivity.)

By portraying Frank struggling through his trials while trying to write a sermon that touches on them, Oliphant takes seriously the tension between lived experience and orthodox teaching. Frank must stand up and preach though his every inclination cuts against the message he knows he is expected to bring.[24] Yet even as Frank wonders if the text of his sermon is really true, doubts the possibility of repentance, and entertains violent fantasies against his enemies, he manages to turn his troubles into a sermon that, like a good parable, "puzzled" his audience: "Somehow the perverse manner in which for once the Curate treated that wicked [older brother] who is generally made so much of in sermons, made his hearers slightly ashamed of themselves" (296). The sermon is both impersonal and personal at once. Frank cannot simply preach as if the truth or untruth of the text did not matter, as if it were an abstract question unconnected with actual human experience in general and the affairs of his own life in particular. He cannot be otherwise than deeply invested in the real metaphysical questions of whether repentance is possible, whether it is worthwhile to try to bring it about, and whether providential justice can be trusted. Neither can he conclude that, because his current crisis seems to set providential justice at naught, such justice must be chimerical. It is this sense of investment in the questions brought on by his predicament that lends the sermon a "thrill of human feeling" that the congregation responds to, however briefly (293). In Wharfside, among the poor flock he serves at a makeshift chapel, the same sermon "drew tears from the eyes of his more open-hearted hearers, who did not think of the proprieties" (297). With both congregations, the fact of Frank's genuine human struggle with his beliefs and his circumstances serves to touch his auditors, even though his discourse is not self-revelatory in content.

Frank's sermon is the first specific instance that reveals his response to the problem of providential justice that his situation presents to him vis-à-vis the parable of the prodigal son. In it, I suggest, we see that Frank struggles seriously with the problem, resisting equally both of the two easiest ways of dismissing it: he neither rejects the truth of the Christian teaching nor denies the reality of his own contrary experience. Rather, he allows both sides of the question to hang suspended in his mind, refusing artificial resolution. In the meantime, Frank is not dramatic enough or self-important enough to imagine that his bitter doubts about providential justice constitute a "crisis" of personal faith. The pressures of his day-to-day life keep him from dwelling on the esoteric theological questions he was forced to address when writing his sermon. However, the questions are still moving in the back of his mind, as is apparent in the critical conversation with Gerald, only three days after the Sunday we have just been considering. In that conversation, the most explicitly theological moment in the novel, Frank directly articulates his hard-won sense of being willing to live with the mystery of faith in providential justice, however inscrutable that justice may be.

In an unusually poignant and unironic passage, Oliphant describes Frank's sympathy with unexplained suffering: "The heart of the Curate ached to think how many problems lay in the darkness, over which the sky stretched silent, making no sign. There were the sorrowful of the earth, enduring their afflictions, lifting up pitiful hands, demanding of God in their bereavements and in their miseries the reason why" (436). Frank refutes the reasoning that led Gerald to convert to Roman Catholicism by saying that the relative indeterminacy of Protestant ("English") theology, as opposed to the "certainty" Gerald craves in Catholicism, accords better with the irresolvable mystery that attends human affairs. Frank asks,

> Can your Church explain why one man is happy and another miserable? – why one has everything and abounds, and the other loses all that is most precious in life? My sister Mary, for example ... she seems to bear the cross for our family. Her children die and yours live. Can you explain to her why? I have heard her cry out to God to know the reason, and He made no answer. ... [O]utside lies a world in which every event is an enigma, where nothing that comes offers any explanation of itself; where God does not show Himself always kind, but by times awful, terrible, a God who smites and does not spare. It is easy to make a harmonious balance of doctrine; but where is the interpretation of life? (436)

Since such existential questions can never be satisfactorily answered by theological theories, they must remain mysterious and indeterminate. The only possible answer, the brothers agree, is to "Trust God," and Frank declares himself "content to take my doctrines on the same terms" of irresolution (436–37).

The echoes of Oliphant's own tortured reflections following her daughter's death suggest that in this remarkable deliverance of Frank, Oliphant is expressing her own unanswerable perplexity. At any rate it is clear from the *Autobiography* that she saw herself as one of those pitied by the curate, "enduring their afflictions ... demanding of God in their bereavements and in their miseries the reason why." She too had asked why her children were taken when others' children lived, and had protested that her dutiful conduct should deserve better from God, though knowing that the latter claim was fallacious.

In addition to closing off the subplot about Gerald, this conversation unfolds the provisional results of Frank's earlier meditations about the injustice of his condition. Frank's ministrations to Gerald require him to verbalize what he has just been discovering over the previous week, namely, that there is no answer to the question of why some people suffer and others thrive, and that any theological system must therefore leave room for unexplained mysteries. Frank here reflects the identical combination of bewilderment and faith to which Oliphant testifies in the early pages of the *Autobiography* and elsewhere: God, being God, does not owe humanity an explanation of his management of affairs. Humans can ask questions, but the only available answer is to trust God.

This conversation also shows that Frank's wrestling over the sermon text, and his resistance to the conventional interpretation of the parable, has not hindered but rather enhanced his ability to function as the "predestined priest of the family" (437). Frank's sense of "the hardness of his own position ... pressing at the moment" (436) heightens his sympathy with suffering and humbles him before the mystery it entails. By the morning, smugness has returned, especially after he receives a letter of support and friendship from Lucy: Frank "pleas[es] himself with those maxims about the ultimate prevalence of justice and truth, which make it apparent that goodness is always victorious, and wickedness punished, in the end. Somehow even a popular fallacy has an aspect of truth when it suits one's own case" (440). This return to the ironic register does not undo the idealism of Frank's priestly ministrations to Gerald the night before. Rather, it chiefly suggests that Frank is more ridiculous in his "slight shade of self-content," in which he feels convinced of providential justice on his behalf, than in his midnight pity and perplexity, when his own position seemed less happy (440).

I have been showing that in Frank's sermon and his conversation with Gerald, Oliphant narrates a tentative but positive resolution of the dilemma of providential justice faced by Frank in his personal life and in his ministry. By not allowing Frank either to lose his faith in response to his sufferings or to deny his experience in favor of platitudes, Oliphant privileges Frank's approach of remaining faithful in light of the mystery with an attitude that combines not taking himself too seriously, feeling compassion for other sufferers, and refraining from dogmatic pronouncements about inscrutable matters. This is very close to the attitude that Oliphant herself seems to have aspired to and in some measure attained.[25] Crucially, Oliphant's rejection of moralistic platitudes about the rewards of goodness remains nevertheless ethically charged: the apparent injustice of the world leads Frank not to the death of God and the abandonment of Christian morality, but rather to increased humility in the face of mystery and, correlatively, to heightened compassion for others.

*****

Having seen Frank through his difficulties in the role of the older brother, Oliphant winds up the prodigal-son subplot of *The Perpetual Curate* with an even more unexpected reversal that pushes several characters towards limit-experience imagined as humility, repentance, forgiveness, and goodwill. As Jack drops his pretense of repentance and declares his intention of "returning to the world" (502), he scathingly turns the tables on his aunts by pointing to the injustice entailed in their pious reception of him according to the rubric of the parable:

> There is my brother Frank, who has been carrying other people about on his shoulders, and doing his duty; but I don't see that you good people are at all moved on his behalf. You leave him to fight his way by himself, and confer your benefits elsewhere, which is an odd sort of lesson for a worldling like me. (501)

Jack taunts them that if he had gone a little further with his humbug, Leonora would have been happy to give the family living to him; yet she persisted in denying it to the dutiful Frank. As he concludes, "that's the way you good people treat a man who never did anything to be ashamed of in his life; and you expect me to give up my evil courses after such a lesson?" (501–02), Jack mocks his aunts for thwarting their own agenda of converting him. Though he celebrates his success in securing "the reward of wickedness," his speech is also, and paradoxically, a back-handed protest against his aunts' injustice, as well as being on some level a decent gesture to help set Frank in his proper place now that Jack is done making fools of everyone.

Precisely as Jack announces his continued rebellion and prodigality, he delivers an effective – and thoroughly orthodox – shaft of reproach against his aunts' religiosity, his brother's potential self-righteousness, and even his own selfishness. The effectiveness of Jack's prophetic reproach can be seen in the strong and uncharacteristic reactions of his hearers, including the squire, Frank, Leonora, and even Jack himself. From the reactions of these characters, we see that by refusing to perform like the penitent prodigal, Jack makes his performance work as a parable. In other words, this scene, like the conclusion to *The Heir of Redclyffe*, reverses the reversal of the parable: while Yonge had the Pharisee unexpectedly become the publican, Oliphant has the unrepentant prodigal unexpectedly act with a moral integrity denied to the religious characters. As in Yonge's book, Oliphant's reversal introduces extravagance into the plot, and that extravagance has transformative effects.

Mr. Wentworth approves of his disgraced son's common sense, and speaks that approval, mingled with regret at Jack's other behavior, in a tone that touches Jack unexpectedly: Jack "was still less prepared to discover the unexpected and inevitable sequence with which one good sentiment leads to another" (503). Calling the squire "father . . . unawares, for the first time in ten years," he offers to relinquish his inheritance in favor of the other children. When the squire refuses, saying he expects Jack to do his duty, not shirk it, Jack ventures that perhaps "I shall not turn out such a scoundrel as – as I ought to do" (504) when he inherits. Even Jack is startled by his own susceptibility to the finer feelings of and for his family. Mr. Wentworth's bluff affection and rebuke has a stronger effect on Jack's morality than the aunts' unjustified partiality.

As for Leonora, Jack's pronouncement has the effect of a parable on her, confronting her with the limitations of her Evangelical moral and theological conventionalities. With Jack's speech:

> an utterly novel and unexpected incident had befallen Miss Leonora: a man of no principles at all had delivered his opinion upon her conduct – and so far from finding his criticism contemptible . . . she had found it true, and by means of it had for perhaps the first time in her life seen herself as others saw her. (505)

Leonora's imperviousness to self-doubt is shaken to the foundations by Jack's performance and the perverse "moral" he draws from it. The result in this honest Evangelical is painful self-analysis under the "rapidly maturing influences of mortification and humbled self-regard": "being a woman of very distinct and uncompromising vision, she could not conceal from herself . . . her own mixed and doubtful motives" (524). Jack's farce of the parable, in other words, exposes to Leonora the hollowness of her Pharisaical religiosity and the weakness of her much-vaunted "principles." Jack's anti-parable is a parable to Leonora.

To Frank, Jack's performance is another sort of parable. Frank receives its "moral" quite literally. His own recent experience has taught him that, in fact, that "it was chiefly the impatient and undutiful who secured their happiness" (481). Jack's worldly counsel, that "the man who gets his own way is the man who takes it" (502), in effect frees Frank to apply this experience by adopting "the prodigal's maxim" for himself, and he determines to marry Lucy without more income than his perpetual curacy (507). Frank waves aside Mary's warning that such disregard for financial prudence would result in debt unbecoming a clergyman. As Frank stingingly tells Lucy when urging her to a prompt marriage, "Providence does not inevitably reward [a patient man] after he has been tried, as we used to suppose" (511). The word "inevitably" suggests that Frank's speech is not a denial of providential justice per se, but rather of the priggishness or Pharisaism (the "slight shade of self-content") associated with assuming that God is bound to vindicate the dutiful, and in particular oneself. Frank's determination not to wait patiently for God to reward his patience, but rather to become a prodigal himself if necessary, is the final reversal that saves Frank from most of the priggishness and presumption that makes the older brother of the parable so obnoxious. In effect, with this move Frank gives up thinking that he deserves a young kid as a reward for his virtue and prepares instead to kill a fatted calf that is not his. By rejecting the role of the upright older brother and assuming the role of the prodigal, Frank acquires some of the freshness of a scapegrace and loses the solemnity of one who unfailingly does the responsible thing.

Nevertheless, the outcome of the narrative balks Frank in his prodigality by an extravagant exertion of (authorial) providential justice on his behalf, when Mr. Morgan decides to take another living and requests that All-Soul's appoint Frank as Rector of Carlingford. This "coming to an end like a trashy novel," as Leonora puts it, leads Leonora to mock, "You are fit to be put in a Good-child series, Frank, as an illustration of the reward of virtue" (535). This rebuke loses its sting, however, as a result of Frank's having scorned to presume upon providence in this way, and because of the fact that, as Frank good-naturedly reminds her, Leonora has done everything possible to prevent his enjoying any sort of happy ending.

In two ways, then, Oliphant's conclusion veers back towards the orthodoxy her narrative has unsettled. First, the assertion of providential justice occurs in spite of the narrator's repeated refusal to rely upon it. The narrator is prepared to mock the idea "that Providence was bound to provide for two good young people who wanted to marry" and professes to not to have "faith in the rewards of virtue which come convenient in such an emergency" (523). Nevertheless, she continues, "it is only pure fiction which can keep true to nature, and weave its narrative in analogy with the ordinary course of life – whereas history demands exactness in matters of *fact*, which are seldom true to nature or amenable to any general rule of existence" (523). Oliphant somewhat awkwardly appeals to the conventional demand of hyper-realism to warrant being, for once, unrealistic – real life does occasionally provide evidence of providential justice. This self-conscious refusal of the topos that she is in fact using is analogous to the position she took with respect to the theological question of providential justice: she knows that the common platitudes about God's providence are not borne out by human experience, but she believes in the wisdom and goodness of God's actions nevertheless.

Second, Jack's subversion of the parable is made to serve orthodox ends, even to his own discomfiture. Jack disingenuously adopts the role of the returned prodigal and uses it to manipulate others for idle amusement. But it is his subversion of the prodigal son plot – his refusal to play the role straight, as written – that does the most effective moral heavy lifting of the novel: rebuking Leonora's Pharisaism, exposing the hollowness of Dora's platitudes, calling for justice to be done to Frank, and even disturbing Jack's own selfish equanimity. In other words, the reversal occasions the extravagance that results in moral transformation. As Jack for once does justice to Frank, Leonora also for once experiences humility and repentance, the squire forgives his son, and Jack expresses hope for his own reform. These effects are of varying strength and persistence, and all are tinged with irony. But they constitute a meaningful expression of limit-experience within the bounds of realist fiction, or of the extraordinary in the ordinary.

Like Jack's reversal of the role of the prodigal son, Oliphant's subversion of the parable draws attention not only to its radical disturbance of normative moral assumptions, but also to the unsettling mystery of divine providence evoked by it. Oliphant exploits the gaps in the parable to imagine alternatives to the conventional interpretations, and this process is highly suitable for her project of thinking through aspects of Christianity that must, she believes, remain indeterminate.

*****

Oliphant's final word on the subjects of waywardness, eternal forgiveness, and justice appears in her late supernatural tale, "The Land of Suspense," written with obvious reference to Cyril but after the deaths of both her sons.[26] In it the nameless young man, who had fallen to various temptations of the flesh but "never with any blasphemous meaning, never defying God," finds himself in a beautiful, happy place (143). He soon realizes, however, that he is without a body and is invisible to others, including his father and other family members who predeceased him. Though he can move freely about the land and speak to others, he is unable to enter the home where his family lives and watches for him hopefully. At first the young man resents this limitation, which he regards as unworthy of God.

> He remembered himself of all the dear stories of his youth, of him whom his father saw afar off and rushed to meet him, not waiting for the confession that was on his lips. And that was hitherto how it had happened to him: and here, where he now was, was not this, the most mercifullest place of all, where everything was love and forgiveness? (138)

He wonders bitterly how the forgiveness of God can be less generous than the forgiveness of his mother, who had always given him the reception of the prodigal in the parable:

> He, whose coming back had always been with joy, even when it came with tears, before whom every door had been thrown open, and whom all about him had thanked with wistful looks for coming home: but now he was shut out. (137)

The self-absorbed young man exploits the sentimental reading of the parable in which the returning prodigal is valorized simply for his return, regardless of his penitence or lack thereof.

Oliphant keenly suggests that this reading, beloved of the parents of wayward children, is adopted presumptuously by those erring ones themselves, who consider themselves entitled to the fatted calf whenever they should condescend to visit their parent. This young man, tellingly, is used to being "thanked" for coming home, though he comes from his follies and with every intention of returning to them. The expectation that the loving parent will interrupt the son's confession is quite convenient for the prodigal who has no real intention of making one. As the spoiled prodigals of *The Perpetual Curate* also suggest, the "straight" or familiar reading of the parable is the stuff of self-indulgent sentimentality, and it runs the risk of compromising justice.

If the familiar reading of the parable actually exacerbates the problem of prodigality (taking prodigality as a synecdoche for moral waywardness generally), then the solution comes in a further reversal of the parable. The turning point occurs for the young man when he sees his brother, who is not disembodied like he is, welcomed by his father and family into their home. Now like the older brother in the parable, the young man sees and resents the welcome given to the other brother while he remains outside. However, in this case the one who is received is the one whose sins are less egregious and whose repentance is whole-hearted. The righteous one is welcomed and the prodigal is left outside – the demands of justice are met at last.

Eventually the young man brings himself to recognize God's justice as well as the extent of the mercy he has in fact received:

> I know . . . that it was not fit that I who had sinned should be rewarded. I have come to little harm. I suffer nothing. I have the whole world left, more beautiful than heart had conceived. And once in a thousand years the Lord will pass by, and I shall see him, even if it be no more. And they will all come to comfort me and talk to me, and not forget me. (154)

With this "manful" recognition of the true state of things, the young man's resentment evaporates into gratitude which suddenly brings with it an overwhelming compassion for his mother, who is now left behind alone on earth. The young man's salvation comes out of his all-consuming, self-effacing prayer for her relief: "he forgot all his troubles and complaining, and became all one prayer, one cry for another, for one who was desolate and had now no child" (154). A day and night of yearning prayer finds the young man endowed with a body out of regard for his love for another.

This last episode is perhaps embarrassing wish-fulfillment on Oliphant's part: the story ends with a note that the son's prayer is still unanswered. However, her story manages to suggest that God's justice, though not transparent on earth, is ultimately effected in comprehensible ways that satisfy both the human yearning for justice and the human need for forgiveness. Free from the demands of realism in this supernatural tale, Oliphant can speculate more widely about the mysterious relation of divine justice and divine mercy, and it is fitting that in doing so she should return to the parable that had both supported and challenged her thinking on this subject so often before.

Whereas Yonge's starting point for rewriting parables is a self-conscious and articulated theological and moral tradition, Oliphant's starting point is her affective and even visceral reactions to existential struggles with which her life confronted her. Both authors, however, find in parables a form and an idiom for simultaneously challenging casual or platitudinous religious conventions and for affirming distinctively Christian truth claims about the nature of God, the power of forgiveness, and the possibility of repentance. Oliphant's affirmations in her realist fiction are slighter than Yonge's: no reader of *The Heir of Redclyffe* can fail to notice the dramatic portrayal of repentance and forgiveness, whereas the undercurrent of Frank's struggle against the apparent injustice of God in *The Perpetual Curate* is easily overlooked. But read alongside the *Autobiography* and other works like "The Open Door" and "The Land of Suspense," *The Perpetual Curate* shows the same urgent consideration of Oliphant's "continual appeal ... to heaven and earth" for the demands of justice and mercy to be reconciled. That appeal, when it takes fictional form, seems to be best expressed in the parabolic mode.

# 5

# "The Agent of a Superior": Stewardship Parables in *Our Mutual Friend*

If Charlotte Yonge is chiefly concerned with upholding a mode of strenuous ethical reflection against popular moral complacency, and Margaret Oliphant is principally focused on mediating existential dilemmas of divine justice, Charles Dickens's preoccupations seem to lie with the public and social consequences of inward moral dispositions. No less than Oliphant and Yonge, however, Dickens's approach to these matters is both formally and existentially indebted to the synoptic parables. In fact, no nineteenth-century British author has been more often described as a parabolist than Charles Dickens. Dickens's blend of realism with the romantic, sentimental, fantastic, and grotesque – and the moral urgency with which it is all imbued – has long fascinated his readers. Critics have characterized this blend in a wide variety of ways, parable prominent among them. While these critics do capture something important about Dickens's narrative project, they generally fail to provide a taut theory of parable on which to hang their analyses. One result of this failure is that, while they often contribute important insights into the texts under examination, those insights regularly get misdirected to the question of whether or not the hopeful, idealistic, and fantastic elements of the novels are somehow sufficient to offset or recuperate the gritty realism of Dickens's portrayals of society's problems. I suggest instead that when we take account of the role of the biblical parables in heralding the kingdom of God, a kingdom paradoxically described in Christian theology as being both a present reality and a future hope, we can see parable as an answer to the otherwise irreconcilable tension of the realist social critic's pessimism at the condition of the world and the believer's transcendent hope in ultimate redemption. This conceptualization makes intelligible the very dynamic we find in Dickens, namely that "Dickens the social critic, and Dickens the myth-maker ... are one" (Hornbeck 1). As G. K. Chesterton has it, Dickens "was delighted at the same moment that he was desperate. The two opposite things existed in him simultaneously, and each in its full strength.... His soul was like a shot silk ... of misery and joy" (37). This tension operates in *Our Mutual Friend* (1865) through the novel's complex engagement with the stewardship parables, found largely in Luke 12.

The inimitable fusion of modes found in Dickens's fiction has been variously described. J. Hillis Miller refers to the "complex interaction of the imaginary and real, in which each sustains and negates the other" (*Form* 105). John Kucich uses a semantic approach to "explain the general, impossible compatibility of the real and the unreal, the meaningful and the non-meaningful, that most readers sense in different phases of Dickens' novels" (187). Bert Hornbeck writes that "Dickens's vision is double: it is realistic, though often in an exaggerated way, as a picture of the world as it is; and it is mythic as an interpretation of this world as a universal context" (1). For Janet Larson, in her study of biblical allusion in Dickens, the author exhibits a tension between the soberly realist mode of Ecclesiastes and the triumphalistic mode of Apocalypse. Combined with Dickens's palpable moral urgency, this juxtaposing of the modes of realism and antirealism points towards the genre of parable.

In his own time Dickens was frequently described in such terms. Dean Arthur Stanley's Westminster Abby memorial sermon on Dickens, for example, praised Dickens as a parabolist like Christ, as did James Panton Ham of Essex Street Chapel. Critics such as Nancy Klenk Hill, Jennifer Gribble, and Janet Larson have followed suit with varying degrees of precision.[1] However, when we examine what these individuals mean when they describe Dickens's fiction as parabolic, we frequently find that parable is but one of the terms used – along with fable, exemplary tale, and myth – to gesture towards the transcendental antirealism that seems to anchor Dickens's critique of the social order around him. Dickens's own contradictoriness and indecision towards formal Christianity tends to defeat those who would find a coherent religious vision in his fiction.[2] The result is that discussions of parable in Dickens rarely go beyond what is essentially a metaphorical or gestural usage of the word.

Both Stanley's and Ham's memorial sermons reach for loose synonyms that blunt the force of the distinctiveness of parable: Ham calls Jesus "a divine fabulist – an inventor of moral stories" in a flabby reduction of parable to exemplary tale (3). Stanley glosses "speaking in parables" as "addressing mankind through romance, novel, tale, and fable" (145) – in other words, parables are nothing more or less than moral instruction offered by means of narrative. What this elides, as we have seen, is the distinctively confrontational content of the instruction offered through narrative, and the distinctive potentialities of the parable genre to generate readers' unique hermeneutical processes. Consequently, Ham's sentimentalized discussion of parables suggests that the parables of both Jesus and Dickens were always comforting to the good (like his audience) and scathing only to the bad (including hypocritical and "professional" clerics [16]). Ham's idea of parable is an exemplary or moral tale that affirms the conventional and complacent notions of the goodness of those who think themselves religious in the right ways, rather than the unsettling disruption of such notions.

The most sustained discussion of parables in Dickens comes in Janet Larson's detailed *Dickens and the Broken Scripture*, which traces Dickens's use of biblical and Prayer-Book allusions through five key novels. Larson is right to complicate Dickens's use of allusions with regard to their stable ironies (in which the Bible serves as a ground of normativity to critique society) and their unstable ironies, in which Dickens's allusions serve to undercut the New Testament certainties they invoke. In this vein she reads *Bleak House* productively in dialogue with Job and Esther, and *Oliver Twist* as providing multiple twists on the parable of the Good Samaritan as well as on Bunyan's tropes of the pilgrim's progress. Yet in spite of a promising description of parable early in the book, Larson comes to use parable to mean simply a story with a latent meaning, and she especially likes to use the phrase "dark parable" as a shorthand for any Dickens narrative that leaves its readers without reassurance in the face of society's failure to take care of the poor and vulnerable. This usage leads her to think of parables as straightforward didactic messages rather than the complex hermeneutical challenges that they are: she refers, for example, to "the didactic parabler's narrowest purposes" (35), and finds that "in his later fiction, [Dickens's] awareness of moral problems arising from the subjectivity of all human interpretation remains in tension with his persisting desire as moral parabler for the legible, objectified design" (120). Larson implies here that the "moral parabler" is at the opposite pole from the "awareness of the subjectivity of all human interpretation."

This limitation of vocabulary is not merely semantic. Rather, it reflects Larson's tendency to flatten the biblical texts she refers to in order to make Dickens's appropriations or subversions stand out from them in higher relief. It also reflects her tendency to overplay her hand: to find in Dickens an infinite regress of contradictions that go farther and farther from the "stable" center of hermeneutical certainty. In contrast, Michael Wheeler has shown that Dickens's theology and uses of biblical language reflect a fairly stable liberal Broad Churchmanship, and Gary Colledge has convincingly argued for "the consistency of his Christian worldview" in terms of essential New Testament values (19).[3] To characterize Dickens's theology as altogether unstable is as much of a mistake as to characterize it as thoroughly orthodox.

In what follows I go beyond such untheorized notions of parable to suggest that a more precise examination of how the specific genre of parable interacts with Dickens's realism will allow us to accurately nuance the blend of idealist Christian hope and realist devastation that is offered throughout his oeuvre, and perhaps most uncompromisingly in his final completed novel. Critics interested in the ethical and religious aspects of Dickens's work are frequently concerned with the balance of the positive, idealist, or life-affirming aspects of a text in comparison with the grim realism with which Dickens portrays social conditions in need of reform. They typically trace a progression from the early novels, in which the ideal is triumphant, to the late novels, in which the realistic portrayal of failures in the social body overpowers the idealistic affirmation of the survival of the good. Whether the pivot is located at *Bleak House*, as Barry Qualls has it, or at *Little Dorrit*, as Janet Larson has it, most critics agree that by the time of *Our Mutual Friend* Dickens's buoyant hopefulness is defeated by the social conditions he anatomizes. Consequently, one of the critical remarks most frequently made about *Our Mutual Friend* is that Dickens's negative portrayal of the city's wretchedness and Society's hollowness quells the hopeful glimmers of the plots relating to the Boffins, the Harmons, Eugene Wrayburn, and Twemlow. The Wrayburn-Headstone plot, with its steady look at variations on human depravity, seems to overpower the novel's closing gestures towards a localized redemption in the Boffin-Harmon family circle. Many readers have found the attempted recuperation of all this filth to be unconvincing, and have doubted Dickens's credence in his own fabulous resolutions.

Such conclusions seem to me unsatisfactory. First, there is the difficulty of quantifying degrees of such things as hope and despair, or optimism and pessimism, or coherence and fragmentation. Even more problematic is the inescapable subjectivity by which one decides how much of one it takes to outweigh the other, or at what point the balance tips from, say, coherence ascendant, to equilibrium between coherence and fragmentation, to fragmentation ascendant. The alternative view I will be proposing does not rely on intuitive judgments like these, because it sees the coexistence of both dispositions as precisely the point. I am less interested in proving that either hope or despair, idealism or realism, prevails over the other, and more interested in seeing the survival of the tension between them – the intensity of the pull in both directions at the same time – as the principal achievement. As we saw in Chapter 2, parables depend for their effect on dramatically juxtaposing the extraordinary with the ordinary, or the ideal with the everyday. The point is never that the ordinary ceases to exist, but that human experience is potentially redescribed through the disorientation that results from imagining extraordinary and extravagant responses to the ordinary failures of individuals and societies. The framework of parable thus gives us another way of looking at the tension between a devastated reality and a sublime ideal that does not depend on a preponderance of empirical evidence for either. Such a framework is especially instructive for a reading of *Our Mutual Friend*, which has been called the "most iconographically Christian of all Dickens's novels" (Nord 36).

\*\*\*\*\*

The appropriateness of regarding *Our Mutual Friend* in light of the genre of parable can be established with reference to Dickens's overt and covert allusions as well as to his use of the narrative strategy of a reversal leading to moral confrontation. On the latter point, we should note that in *Our Mutual Friend*, characters persistently understand their own stories with reference to other stories. The etymological meaning of *parabole*, throwing alongside, suggests that parables are stories that are laid alongside other stories in order to make visible aspects of those stories, or to intervene in them in some way. Bella recreates the meal of the Three Hobgoblins, Rogue Riderhood turns into a Wolf, Jenny Wren as Cinderella requests transformations by her fairy godmother Riah, and Mr. Boffin pretends to emulate the illustrious misers. Fantastic stories are invoked to illuminate, recall, challenge, and reconfigure the stories the characters are living. This parabolic function, as some critics have noticed, is extended to the reader, who is asked implicitly to lay the story of *Our Mutual Friend* in some way alongside her own.

As we have seen in other parables and retellings of parables, in *Our Mutual Friend* moral growth occurs as a result of self-knowledge, and self-knowledge comes from seeing one's own actions externally dramatized in the form of a story. The most direct biblical model is Nathan's parable of the ewe lamb in 2 Samuel. Likewise, the major moral developments of characters in *Our Mutual Friend* occur in relation to such external dramatization of characters' actions and attitudes. Most obviously, Bella's reformation is effected by Mr. Boffin's apparent celebration of unvarnished greed. As Bella later expresses it (referring to herself in the third person), "[Y]ou showed her, in yourself, the most detestable sides of wealth, saying in your own mind, 'This shallow creature would never work the truth out of her own weak soul, if she had a hundred years to do it in; but a glaring instance kept before her may open even her eyes and set her thinking'" (754). Boffin makes himself a parable, reflecting Bella's attitudes back to herself, so that she can see her own "weak soul" and remedy it. As we have seen throughout this study, the signature achievement of parables is to open one's eyes and set one thinking. Bella's story is not the only such instance in the novel, though it is the most obvious. A number of characters, including Riah, Sophronia Lammle, and Mr. Venus, come to understand the stakes of their ethical dilemmas from the self-knowledge that results from, as Riah puts it, "seeing the whole thing visibly presented as upon a theatre" (708).

This pattern of moral transformation arising from seeing one's own actions in the light of a story about someone else is extended to the reader. Rosemary Mundhenk shows that Dickens's withholding of information from the reader, specifically regarding the "pious fraud" by which Boffin accomplishes the reform of Bella, challenges the reader's confidence in his or her judgments of characters. Though Mundhenk does not use the word parable to name the narrative strategy she uncovers, her account of Dickens's use of this reversal aptly describes parabolic effect. Dickens takes in the reader just as Boffin takes in Bella, and with a similar effect of facilitating self-knowledge. Arguing against those readers who have accused Dickens of changing his mind mid-stream about Boffin's character, Mundhenk demonstrates that the surprise reversal was key to Dickens's conception of this subplot. As John Reed observes, "The narrator withholds information that tests the reader's assessments of characters, therefore implying a warning against rash judgment" (*Dickens and Thackeray* 301). This strategy, moreover, tricks the reader into making excessively severe moral judgments of the characters, thus "promoting a self-correcting impulse in the reader that reinforces the novel's message of restraint" (*Dickens and Thackeray* 301). This withholding of information to mislead the reader's sympathy is much like what we saw in Yonge's *The Heir of Redclyffe*, which similarly induces skepticism about one's ability to judge one's own or another's moral state.

Similarly, Audrey Jaffe writes that "it is precisely at the moment of surprise, when we become aware of how misled we have been, that we glimpse the potential depth of our insecurity.... Revelation, then, comes with a double force, the force not just of a solution but of one's own epistemological limitations" (162). As Eugene turns on his pursuer Headstone, so the text turns on the reader:

> This scene dramatizes the moment of surprise as a demonstration of knowledge by means of peripety, or reversibility. In so doing, it also dramatizes the moment at which the text turns on the reader – or we might say, looks at its reader, taking him or her by surprise – and readers who have considered themselves omniscient find that they have been misled, exposed, taken in. (165–66)[4]

Dickens's use of this strategy of reversal to challenge the reader's moral and epistemological certainty justifies us in saying that *Our Mutual Friend* is deeply invested in the narrative economy of parable as I understand it in this study. *Our Mutual Friend* is parabolic not merely because it uses a story to impart moral instruction, as Stanley and Ham would have it, but because it uses a story to confront the reader with the inadequacy of his or her self-complacent certainty about who the good guys and the bad guys are.

Besides narrative strategy generally, parables are important as particular reference points within the text of *Our Mutual Friend*. References to Jesus's parables rise to the surface of the narrative in a few key and easily recognized instances. Unlike Oliphant's works, however, *Our Mutual Friend* does not follow a single parable. Nor does Dickens have a self-conscious and finely-tuned theory of parable like we saw in Charlotte Yonge.[5] Rather, simultaneously invoking several parables that focus on questions of money, *Our Mutual Friend* turns the parables around in multiple ways in the different plots. In fact, Dickens's novel suggests most dramatically the potentialities of reinscribing a parable in a complex, multiplot fiction: each treatment of the parabolic material allows for a different refraction of its tensions or a different kind of reversal of expectations. As some critics have noticed, the parable of the prodigal son is inverted in various plots within the novel.[6] While these will form part of the discussion to follow, I am most interested in tracing the novel's more pervasive but less visible engagement with figures and incidents drawn from a cluster of parables pertaining to stewardship. Appearing together in Luke 12, the parables of the rich fool, the alert servants, and the wise and foolish stewards provide a sustained commentary on the use of resources in the context of cosmic time. The thematically related parables of the talents (Matthew 25) and the pounds (Luke 19), in which sums of money are given to servants to manage while the master is away, also lie in the background of *Our Mutual Friend*. Finally, we will see that the parables of the alert servants and of the talents and the pounds point to the apocalyptic import of the stewardship parables.

The parable that is most frequently associated with *Our Mutual Friend* is that of the prodigal son, and for good reason. Variations on the prodigal son appear in no fewer than four of the novel's configurations of characters: Jenny Wren and her father Mr. Cleaver, Charley and Gaffer Wexam, Old Harmon and John Harmon, and

Eugene and his "M.R.F." In all cases but the last, the parable is inverted in wrenching ways. Instead of the satisfying tale of the beloved lost son returned to the loving father, which the Victorians saw as emblematic of the whole gospel message, Dickens gives us families sundered unto death by greed, pride, and addiction. Mr. Harmon sends his disinherited son into exile in a foreign land, in a reversal of the son who takes his prematurely bestowed inheritance willfully to abandon his loving father's home. Charley and Gaffer enact a double reversal: Charley deserts his father like the younger son in the parable, but he does so not in order to waste money but to gain it prudently and thereby become "respectable." Ironically, Gaffer calls Charley an "Unnat'ral young beggar!" because Charley prefers schooling to begging. For his part, Gaffer reverses his role as father by his absolute refusal to welcome Charley home, even as a penitent: "Let him never come a nigh me to ask me my forgiveness.... Let him never come within sight of my eyes, nor yet within reach of my arm" (81). In the most pitiful revision of the parable in the novel, Jenny Wren imagines her drunken father as her "prodigal son," wasting the family's meager substance on his riotous living. Mr. Cleaver's death in a drunken stupor, like Gaffer's retributive death while plundering bodies on the Thames and Mr. Harmon's isolated death in his empty house, disallows any reconciliation between these parents and children.

In the face of all these devastating inversions, it is surprising to find one subplot in which the parable ends with something like forgiveness and reconciliation. Eugene Wrayburn is a sort of prodigal son, living profligately off a limited inheritance, accumulating debts, and declining to work at his profession. He keeps his distance from the father he ironically and coolly refers to as "M.R.F." However, after Eugene has taken the virtually unimaginable step of marrying Lizzie, Eugene reports an unexpected reconciliation with his father, who had earlier urged Eugene to make a socially advantageous marriage. During a brief visit, his father suggested that Lizzie should have her portrait painted, which, as Eugene tells Mortimer, "coming from M.R.F., may be considered equivalent to a melodramatic blessing" (790). Eugene continues, "When M.R.F. said that, and followed it up by rolling the claret (for which he called, and I paid), in his mouth, and saying, 'My dear son, why do you drink this trash?' it was tantamount – in him – to a paternal benediction on our union, accompanied with a gush of tears" (790). Mr. Wrayburn turns out to be "a much younger cavalier than" Eugene (790). This unexpected youthfulness and chivalry in M.R.F aligns him with the supposedly "harmless old female" Twemlow, who takes on chivalric honors by his gentlemanly behavior at the novel's conclusion. However understated and ironically narrated, this acceptance of Eugene's marriage by the senior Mr. Wrayburn constitutes the single instance in the novel in which the prodigal-son plot leads to a gesture in the direction of limit-experience: transcendent values – the father's admiration for beauty and courage – prevail over brutal or materialistic ones. That the positive version of the parable is outnumbered three-to-one by the broken versions does not mean that Dickens was soberly realistic when narrating the first three and groundlessly cheerful – haphazardly breaking his own realist codes – when narrating the final one. Rather, it reflects that Dickens's full apprehension of the irretrievable brokenness of most relationships did not keep him from recognizing the possibility that extravagant acts of love and courage like Eugene's and Lizzie's sometimes, as in the parable, lead to restored relationships.

\*\*\*\*\*

As with the prodigal son parable, in which Dickens confounds the roles of parents and children, wrong-doers and well-doers, so in his rendering of the parables of stewardship Dickens turns owners into stewards and stewards into owners. In fact, this interchanging of roles is the thematic crux of the novel's plots about money. The stewardship parables, used unobtrusively but pervasively throughout the novel, supply a conceptual model that enables the transformation of "illth" into wealth (Ruskin's terms). Properties in the hands of stewards make wealth; they are the dust that is really gold, that conduces to life. Conversely, properties in the grip of owners or would-be owners tend to make illth; they are the gold that is really dust that conduces to death.[7]

The parable of the wise steward appears in Luke 12 along with other parables and teachings relating to the use of money. First Jesus tells the parable of the rich fool, who proudly accumulates so much grain that he had to tear down his barns and build bigger ones. He complacently assumes that he can now take life easy, but God tells him, "Thou fool, this night thy soul shall be required of thee: then whose shall those things be, which thou hast provided?"

(12:20). This parable is followed by various exhortations about the use of money, including the following familiar aphorisms: "Provide yourselves ... a treasure in the heavens that faileth not, where no thief approacheth, neither moth corrupteth. For where your treasure is, there will your heart be also" (12:33-34).

Jesus's next speech is the brief parable of the alert servants: when the master comes home late, he rewards those servants who were awake and watching for his return. Specifically, the master is so taken by their faithfulness that he invites them to recline at table while *he* serves *them*. In response to Peter's question as to whether this parable is addressed to the disciples or to all the people, Jesus tells the parable of the wise steward:

> Who then is that faithful and wise steward, whom his lord shall make ruler over his household, to give them their portion of meat in due season? Blessed is that servant, whom his lord when he cometh shall find so doing. Of a truth I say unto you, that he will make him ruler over all that he hath. But if that servant say in his heart, My lord delayeth his coming; and shall begin to beat the menservants and maidens, and to eat and drink, and to be drunken; The lord of that servant will come in a day when he looketh not for him, and at an hour when he is not aware, and will cut him in sunder, and will appoint him his portion with the unbelievers. ... For unto whomsoever much is given, of him shall be much required: and to whom men have committed much, of him they will ask the more. (12:42-48)

In Matthew 25 and Luke 19, a similar tag is attached to the parables of the ten talents and the ten minas, respectively. In those parables, servants are given different amounts of money before the master leaves for a time. The servants who put the money to use and make more money are rewarded with command of more money or cities, and the ones who bury or hide the money to keep it safe are rebuked and deprived of their paltry sums.[8]

While focusing primarily on the parable of the wise and foolish stewards in what follows, I also want to keep these other thematically related parables and exhortations in mind. Old Harmon, a miser, is clearly like the rich fool, accumulating possessions in vast mounds and being tormented by the question of who will inherit his wealth after him. In the characters of Boffin, John Rokesmith/Harmon,

Wegg, and Riah, Dickens presents various alternatives for the relations among stewardship, mastery, and servanthood, constantly problematizing who holds these different roles and how they are held. The plot of Bella's moral development entails her learning to value the otherworldly "treasure in heaven" rather than the filthy lucre she desires at first.

Before proceeding to discuss the way these parabolic elements appear in *Our Mutual Friend*, however, several points should be made about the parables themselves. As understood by nineteenth-century commentators, the concept of stewardship had very wide application to secular life no less than religious life.[9] While a handful of commentators insisted on narrow spiritual readings of the parable of the talents/pounds, regarding the talents as allegorical for spiritual gifts only,[10] most considered that the talents represented both spiritual and material goods.[11] The parable of the stewards received far less exposition – it does not even appear in Trench's often-reprinted commentary on the parables of Jesus. But it is evident from the text of the parable that the stewards are judged on the basis of how their conduct towards others reflects their fidelity to their absent master. Given that this parable was told in response to Peter's question about whether the previous parable (of the alert servants) was directed only at the disciples or at the whole crowd, the parable of the wise and foolish stewards is evidently intended to illustrate the relation between the disciples and the rest of the people with respect to their mutual relation to God. In that light, the parable emphasizes the leaders' responsibility to serve the people and not the other way around. The wise steward "give[s] them their portion of meat in due season" (12:42). The foolish steward, in contrast, "begin[s] to beat the menservants and maidservants" (12:45) while the master is gone. He takes advantage of his position to demand service from others, while the wise steward, like the master in the parable of the alert servants, makes himself the servant of others.

Moreover, the parable of the stewards, like the parable of the pounds, also concerns the temporal control of resources. In the parable of the stewards, these resources are literally represented as the food to be given to the other servants. Not only does the foolish steward act as though the other servants are supposed to serve him, but he also appropriates to himself the resources provided by the master for the benefit of all. Instead of giving the other servants their food, the foolish steward "begin[s] to eat and drink, and to be drunken" (12:45). The faithful steward, who fairly distributes the food to the others, is rewarded by being made "ruler" over the master's whole property. In the parable of the talents, similarly, the money is entrusted to the servants as a way of testing their fitness for future positions of authority.[12] Those who diligently increase the money entrusted to them are appointed as rulers of corresponding numbers of cities. This parable was read by Victorian commentators as underwriting capitalism: God expects his followers to increase their financial holdings by hard work, reasonable risk, and thrift.[13] Yet the capitalism thus authorized is an altered one in which production does not equal ownership. Because the initial capital is bestowed by the master, and the proceeds are to be returned to the master, the accumulation of money is bound to the ethical demands of stewardship indicated in the other parables – namely, the use of goods or power to serve and benefit others. The reward of the "faithful and wise" servants is not more property to call their own, but more goods to manage or govern on behalf of the master, to whom they remain accountable according to the standard given in the previous parable.[14]

These parables, then, artfully blend the themes of the use of money and of pastorship; they are about both the spiritual and temporal governance of the believing community and of its resources. For the purposes of Dickens's novel, the accent of course falls on the secular applications, and this accent was by no means alien even to the explicitly religious exposition of the parables. The most exhaustive commentary of any of these parables by a Victorian divine was James Stirling's 1873 *The Stewardship of Life, or Studies on the Parable of the Talents*. This book, which was well-received in periodicals across the Victorian religious spectrum,[15] posited that that parable's chief applications lie in the secular realm. In the present dispensation, "God no longer appears in the drama of human life" (28). The "beginning of Christianity is the end of miracle . . . . The human steward appears on the field alone, and [history] will see nothing but man in the world" (27–28). The ultimate implication of this parable of stewardship, according to Stirling, is that Christian reformers should apply themselves to the improvement of social conditions, which are formative of individuals' spiritual health: "the sway of the physical nature in the fashioning of character and principle is not sufficiently recognized" by Christians, he chides (247). Readers of his book, Stirling implies, are in a position to use their advantages of means, education, and energy – their "talents" – to improve the material lives of those around them and in that way ease others' journey towards salvation. Likewise the Evangelical William Arnot urges in his commentary on the parable of the talents, "Let each according to his means and opportunity lay himself and his talents out to . . . feed hungry mouths, and cover naked backs, to enlighten dark minds and save perishing souls" (529).

This interpretation clearly accords with Dickens's liberal Christianity, which emphasized the duty of humanitarian charity towards the less fortunate, deemphasized transcendence as a solution to human problems, and insisted strenuously on the responsibility of the governing class to enable the poor's spiritual flourishing by first satisfying temporal needs.[16] As he expressed it in a speech on sanitary reform, the poor man

> is so surrounded by and imbedded in material filth, that his soul cannot rise to the contemplation of the great truths of religion. . . . But give them a glimpse of heaven through a little of its light and air; give them water; help them to be clean; . . . and then they will be brought willingly to hear of Him whose thoughts were so much with the poor, and who had compassion on all human suffering. (*Speeches, Letters, and Sayings* 104)

It would not be an overstatement to say that Dickens's whole oeuvre worries over these concepts and problems. That power is to be exercised only in service to others, that resources are to be distributed equitably, and that social leaders ("pastors" in Lauren Goodlad's terminology) are accountable for how they treat the poor – these are all central tenets of his ethical vision. In a 1842 speech, Dickens stated that his "moral creed" included the belief "that we hold our sympathies, hopes, and energies, *in trust* for the many, not the few" (*Speeches, Letters, and Sayings* 26, emphasis added). Consequently, Dickens's bad characters (and institutions) can all be condemned in terms of their failures of stewardship: witness the poor law's treatment of Oliver, the hard-heartedness of Bounderby, the colossal waste of money and lives generated by Chancery, and the evasion of responsibility by the Barnacles. The parable of the talents is well-suited to carry the moral freight of the ethical convictions requiring what Dickens called "good management and just stewardship" of the nation and empire ("A Haunted House" 483).

*****

The stewardship parables conceptually solve the problem that, according to George Levine, lies at the heart of the realist novel, namely, how to reconcile the protagonist's capitalistic success with his moral virtue. Levine writes, "Novelists need the success of their protagonists to bring off their comic endings, but they are hard pressed to imagine ways, within the textured representation of middle class life and economy, to represent it without radically compromising the protagonists' moral integrity" (*Realism, Ethics and Secularism* 228). The usual symptom of this problem is indecisive, colorless male protagonists, and the usual solution is the device of inheritance. Levine claims that this problem "is exacerbated in *Our Mutual Friend*" and finds its fullest instance in "Harmon's status as 'dead'" (*Dying to Know* 153). However, I suggest that Dickens's use of the parabolic trope of stewardship represents a serious and at least partially successful effort to apply a Christian solution to this basic problem. The twin antidotes to greed, for Dickens as for the gospels, are stewardship and gratitude. With the model of grateful stewardship Dickens is able to imagine capitalistic activity without accompanying corruption.

This dynamic explains why Riah is not morally tainted by the usury and exploitation he engages in on Fledgeby's behalf. Though we might like to see Riah resign over being made to prosecute others mercilessly for debt, in fact he does no such thing. Riah resigns only when he realizes that his complicity with Fledgeby's "little joke" abets vicious anti-Semitic stereotypes. Riah's debt-mongering per se leaves him as morally untainted as Oliver's residence among thieves leaves him. Riah's truthful, though unheeded, claims of nonresponsibility are, as it were, honored by the narrator, who exonerates Riah from the moral stain of cruelty: "I am not the principal here. I am but the agent of a superior, and I have no choice, no power" (559). Moreover, Dickens strives (though unsuccessfully, in the eyes of most modern readers) to invest Riah with positive moral value deriving from his obedience as a steward and the gratitude that motivates him to that obedience. The moral fault in the doings of Pubsey & Co. is all Fledgeby's, both because of his sadistic enjoyment of his power of afflicting others and because of his tyrannical mastery of Riah. The parable of the talents reflects a notion of stewardship that is paradoxically both autonomous and accountable: the servants are not told what to do with the money they are given, but they are held accountable for the results of their use of it (Arnot 527). But Fledgeby micromanages all of his steward's actions, leaves Riah absolutely no room for independent decisions, and literally holds him "accountable for every single bead" (274). Fledgeby's greed and tyranny, like the miserliness of Old Harmon, result in his own injury. Jenny plots for Alfred Lammle to flog the odious Fledgeby, recalling Jesus's words that the foolish steward who "knew his lord's will, and did not . . . do it, shall be beaten with many stripes" (Luke 12:47).

In the case of Riah and Fledgeby, then, we have a stewardship model gone awry, comparable to the prodigal-son stories that did so. Another model of dysfunction can be found in the "Society" circle of the Veneerings and Podsnaps, both of whom presume to the ownership of things they do not in fact own. The Veneerings try to buy social standing through the acquisition of goods and chattels – including, in Dickens's macabre satire, the interchangeable guests who function as domestic implements. The falseness of these mortgaged purchases, by which they desire to appear to own things they do not in fact own, echoes the falseness of the gentility they seek to establish by appearing to be well-connected.

In the Harmon-Boffin plot, stewardship works much more felicitously.[17] Although Dickens's use of it does not altogether overcome the problems that Levine predicts – John inherits his wealth, and he remains one of those weak male protagonists – the novel does make some important headway on these problems. At least, I argue, it is not the case that "In the later Dickens, there is simply no touching money without being dirtied" (Levine, *Realism, Ethics and Secularism* 238). The trope of stewardship, borrowed from the parables, makes it possible for Boffin and Harmon both to thrive without being corrupted by their wealth. Harmon's status as "dead," does not, in the way it is used in the novel, prevent his being active as a "man of business" and even as a suitor to Bella (180). It is also noteworthy that in this plot we do not find the usual bright line between inherited and earned wealth. Old Harmon's wealth is, after all, very largely of Boffin's making, since Boffin was the long-time superintendent of the business. Boffin's inheritance of this property, therefore, is not unearned in the same sense as, say, Pip's inheritance of Magwich's fortune. John, too, is allowed to participate in this labor by working as an unpaid "man of business" for Boffin for a period of time. John learns the business of managing the estate by working as a steward, just as Boffin learned the dust business in his role as steward to John's father.

When "Mr. Rokesmith" offers his service to Mr. Boffin as secretary, Mr. Boffin is puzzled: "we have always believed a Secretary to be a piece of furniture, mostly of mahogany .... Now, you won't think I take a liberty when I mention that you certainly ain't *that*" (180). Unlike several characters in the novel, Mr. Boffin never confuses people for objects or commodities. Rokesmith clarifies that "he had used the word in the sense of Steward," which Mr. Boffin again misunderstands as the attendant on a ship (180). Though comically unfamiliar with the term, Mr. Boffin is eminently acquainted with the concept. His and his wife's own labor provides the original model of stewardship that the book refracts in various ways:

> Through his most inveterate purposes, the dead Jailer of Harmony Jail had known these two faithful servants to be honest and true. So, even while it was his daily declaration that he distrusted all mankind ... he was as certain that these two people, surviving him, would be trustworthy in all things from the greatest to the least, as he was that he must surely die. (105–6)

Dickens's narrative thus juxtaposes the figure of the rich fool, whose sin is "forgetting that he is the steward of [his gains], not the owner," with the figure of the faithful steward (Farrar 742). The Boffins serve a long apprenticeship in stewardship of the Harmon property, proving their fitness to be the executors of Mr. Harmon's will and indeed the heirs of his fortune. Even while waiting for John Harmon's return from abroad, "The room was kept like this, Rokesmith, against the son's return," Mr. Boffin tells his secretary. "In short, everything in the house was kept exactly as it came to us, for him to see and approve" (185). The teasing irony of Mr. Boffin's saying this while escorting that son, in the persona of the secretary Rokesmith, to see the house should not distract us from the revelation that the Boffins continue, as possessors of the house, to hold their ownership at arm's length.

The Boffins, of course, never crave possession of the fortune. The gold that corrupts Harmon in his possession of it never corrupts

Noddy and his "old lady" in their humble management of it. He tells Rokesmith that the single Mound "would have been enough for us . . . in case it had pleased God to spare the last of those two young lives and sorrowful deaths. We didn't want the rest" (185). This declaration is not pious cant: it is corroborated by the revelation at the end of the book that the Boffins had in their possession Old Harmon's last will, disinheriting his son absolutely and leaving the whole property to them. The couple's literally extravagant decision to suppress this will amounts to their choosing to remain as stewards of the son's property rather than claiming the ownership to which the will entitles them.

Even when John Harmon's death is established and the Boffins are legal owners of the property, they retain the habit of regarding themselves in the light of stewards, in part because that role is more conducive to their peace of mind. Boffin declares himself happier in the role of manager than of owner: "When I was foreman at the Bower . . . I considered the business very satisfactory," whereas ownership troubles his mind. "It's a great lot to take care of," he laments to Mortimer Lightwood (94). Lightwood's cynical reminder that others would be happy to take the management of the money upon themselves is no relief to Mr. Boffin, who knows that he would be morally responsible for the actions of his steward as well as for his own. Having a steward would not diminish his responsibility in the way that being a steward does. Mrs. Boffin's plan to adopt a child, give him John's name (not their own), and endow him with the property Mrs. Boffin still refers to as "John's own money," is another way in which the couple maintains a posture of stewardship towards their possessions (330).

The stewardship plot gets more complicated as John Harmon, under the name Rokesmith, becomes secretary (or "Steward," as he says) to Boffin. John, who is thought by both the reader and himself to be the rightful owner of the property, acts as steward to the Boffins, who earlier acted as stewards on behalf of John while awaiting his return. Now John echoes Riah's refrain, telling Headstone on one occasion, "You should know that I am not the principal here" (379). In this role, John "was discerning, discreet, and silent, though as zealous as if the affairs had been his own. He showed no love of patronage or the command of money, but distinctly preferred resigning both to Mr. Boffin. If, in his limited sphere, he sought power, it was the power of knowledge; the power derivable from a perfect comprehension of his business" (193). Most readers will by this point perceive that "Rokesmith" is John Harmon, so the line "as if the affairs had been his own" has ironic resonance. However, we also see that John is using his position as a sort of apprenticeship to learn his affairs thoroughly, all the while conscientiously keeping himself in the position of a steward.

As the plot plays out, further reversals and abdications occur. John considers "coming to life" and asserting (what he believes to be) his rightful ownership, but believing that that action would dispossess his benefactors and would be unwelcome to Bella, he decides against it. Like the unprofitable servant in the parable of the pounds, John is tempted to "bury" himself and his claim to the Harmon property. This apparently safe and altruistic action must not be allowed, for the same reason that the servant is punished for his diffident reluctance to make use of his master's property. As Stirling writes with special relevance for *Our Mutual Friend*, "The [buried] talent is in the wrong place. Dust is an indifferent bank" (92). Harmon's becoming known to the Boffins, though it is not related until much later in the novel, occurs soon after his resolution to bury himself precisely in order to spare him from culpability for such a mistake.

At last, Boffin presents the third and final will, which leaves all the property to himself, in order to deprive Wegg of his power to blackmail Boffin with the second will. However, as a condition of establishing this will Boffin requires John to accept his father's fortune as a gift from himself and his wife. As in the parable, the faithful steward is rewarded by being placed over all his master's possessions. The original faithful steward, Boffin, is given ownership of the property while John is believed dead; then the second faithful steward, John, is given ownership when he comes "back to life." However, even when accepting the title of master de jure, neither considers himself master de facto, but rather each holds himself in the posture of stewardship to the other. So while Harmon is believed dead, Boffin continues to behave like a steward, and when Harmon is fully instated as master, he never forgets that "I owe everything I possess, solely to the disinterestedness, uprightness, tenderness, goodness (there are no words to satisfy me) of Mr. and Mrs. Boffin" (768).

In short, John and the Boffins trade off ownership and stewardship of the property throughout the book, each refusing to appropriate the property as his or their own. These complicated transactions at last bring the long-delayed "satisfactoriness" that, as Boffin mourns, had always been lacking to the Harmon fortune. The fortune is wealth to Mr. and Mrs. Boffin and to John and Bella Harmon because they all steadfastly refuse to own it. Since someone must own it to prevent it from going to sharks like Wegg, Dickens arranges for Harmon, the son and rightful heir, to own it finally, but it comes to him only after his having refused it twice (when he decided to be dead, and then to remain so) and even then only "through the munificence of Mr. Boffin," the legal owner (768). It is no wonder that Bella, in her spirited defense of Harmon against the staged insults of Mr. Boffin, declares to Mr. Boffin, "[T]hroughout I saw in him the master, and I saw in you the man" (586). The roles are traded back and forth until such muddling is inevitable, and designedly so.

Wegg, by contrast, is like the foolish steward of the parable, presuming to own what he in fact does not own. As a servant, Wegg is "constitutionally of a shirking temperament," always trying to get more money for less or no work (191–2). Boffin's mastery of Wegg was of the gentlest: Wegg was overpaid, well fed, and assigned the lightest of labors. Boffin always addressed Wegg as "Mr" and spoke of him respectfully, if absurdly, as his "literary man, *with a wooden leg.*" In the terms of the parable of the wise steward, Boffin abundantly fulfilled his obligation to give the other servant his food at the proper times. Their roles are temporarily reversed when Wegg finds the second will and thinks it gives him power to blackmail Boffin. As Venus puts it, Wegg begins "to dispose of [the] property the moment he knew his power" (565), and Wegg himself says, "Every time I see [Boffin] putting his hand in his pocket, I see him putting it into my pocket. Every time I hear him jingling his money, I hear him taking liberties with my money" (568).

The contrast between Wegg and Boffin is made even more dramatic as we see Wegg not only improperly assume the ownership that Boffin has refused to assume, but also assert tyrannical mastery over a servant. Corresponding to the beatings the foolish steward inflicts on his fellow servants in the parable, Wegg's anticipation of this power has an ominous physical dimension. Wegg tells Venus, "I'll put him in harness, and I'll bear him up tight, and I'll break him and drive him" (570). He even considers himself entitled to physically attack the old man the night that Boffin retrieves the

Dutch bottle from his mound. After revealing the second will to Boffin, Wegg comically and crassly asserts his supposed mastery in every way, beginning with his demand that Boffin "inform that menial [Sloppy] that I am Master here!" (640). Wegg particularly delights in humiliating Boffin by addressing him familiarly, giving him permission to sit down, and ordering him to hold his tongue. Moreover, Wegg places Boffin in the humiliating position of an untrusted steward, demanding full accounting of all Boffin's affairs to be charged against the division of the property under the terms of the blackmail: "Till the Mounds is down and the business completed, you're accountable for all the property, recollect. Consider yourself accountable to me" (645).

Wegg's punishment, then, is doubly appropriate. Not only is he deprived at a stroke of his illusions of ownership by the climactic presentation of the third will, but Sloppy has already punished Wegg's tyranny in kind. When Sloppy, in disguise as a tireless dust contractor, forces Wegg to attend day and night to the rapid removal of the mounds, he turns Wegg's own distrust and greed into scourges. The constitutional shirker for once works like a dog under the direction of "that menial," Sloppy. Wegg's desire to use money to tyrannize over others results in his own slavery and injury, as it did likewise for Old Harmon and Fledgeby.

Just as the trope of the prodigal son concluded positively in the single case of Eugene and his M.R.F., so do the stewardship parables find a brief and surprising conclusion for Eugene and Lizzie. In the same conversation in which Eugene relates his reconciliation with his father, he also tells Mortimer, "With such a guardian and steward beside me, as the preserver of my life . . . the little that I can call my own will be more than it ever has been. It need be more, for you know what it has always been in my hands. Nothing" (790). Eugene's ownership previously resulted in prodigality: his small income was actually worse than nothing, because it "prevent[ed] me from turning to at Anything" (790). With Lizzie as a steward, even Eugene's small property can be wealth and not the illth it has been. Eugene's putting his money in her hands, dissociating himself from ownership and instead invoking the model of stewardship, promises to set even his affairs right at last.

*****

As noted above, much of the criticism of *Our Mutual Friend* reverts to the question of whether the book's hopeful and restorative elements are sufficient to dispel its disturbing realist elements.[18] Is the Boffin-Harmon plot (generally disliked for its melodramatic absurdities of character and plot) an adequate answer to the Wrayburn-Headstone plot (generally liked for its complex characters and realist plot)? The majority of critics have answered that question in the negative. J. Hillis Miller writes that, "Whereas *Bleak House* in the end put an apparently dispersed world back together, *Our Mutual Friend* remains true to its rejection of the idea that there is an ideal unity of the world transcending the differences between individual lives, and perceptible from the outside by Providence or by the omniscient eye of the narrator" (*Charles Dickens* 292). Barbara Hardy's judgment has been often repeated: "Dickens creates such a powerful anatomy of a corrupting and corrupted society, ruled and moved by greed and ambition, that the wish-fulfilling fantasies of virtue and conversion are too fragile to support faith" (25). More recent work does not leave this assumption behind. Lauren Goodlad, agreeing with Mary Poovey, finds that "The Harmons' idyllic union is powerless to rectify the entrenched social problems elsewhere described in more realist terms" (*Victorian Literature* 162). Vincent Newey's extensive discussion of the novel concludes that "Dickens's last finished novel technically cleans up 'decadence' yet really remains its host" (288).[19]

Influential studies of religious motifs in *Our Mutual Friend* have largely inclined to this mordant note. For Barry Qualls, "Dickens is increasingly unable to believe in the transcendental reality that Carlyle always asserts.... [A]fter *Dombey*, the realm of natural supernaturalism becomes more and more a small human society and, finally, something alive – if at all – only in the imagination" (85–86). Janet Larson's analysis culminates in a similar point: "Although Dicken's novel embodies the possibility of provisional solutions in such difficulties, it works mightily towards what John Harmon declares *such* 'a quantity of believing!,' (4.5.755) that we cannot endorse the happy resolutions with the credulity they require, given the darker parables we have read" (283, emphasis in original). Larson continues, "But as 'once upon a time' casts out 'These times of ours,' Dickens thwarts his own serious intentions by locating his ideal outside the actualities of a novel he has himself problematized" (300). For these critics the failure of *Our Mutual*

*Friend* to overcome its own darkness indicates Dickens's failure, as it were in spite of himself, to hold onto Christian faith and hope.

A minority view regards the hopeful elements of the text as prevailing over the dark elements. In U. C. Knoeflmacher's reading of the novel's tension between "despair" and "laughter," the realist impulse to despair is dispelled by Dickens' stubborn faith in "an 'eternal law' based on the heart" (167). The "comic reversal" of the novel's conclusion deploys the "illogical logic of nursery rhymes and fairy tales," resolving the novel on a positive note by authorial sleight-of-hand (164).[20] Bert Hornbeck maintains that the ending establishes some solid ground of hope vis-à-vis Twemlow and Eugene and even a revived Mortimer, who stands by his convictions in defiance of Society. According to Andrew Sanders, despite the "pervasive social demoralization" of the world of *Our Mutual Friend*, "Dickens nevertheless maintains his faith in human survival through an exposition of the destinies of those major characters who, with due grace, embody a redemptive process and manage to rise above a general dehumanisation" (174).

I have already indicated why I find this dispute unprofitable. A better approach can be found by recognizing that Dickens's use of parables enables precisely the coexistence of persistent hope in the face of pervasive corruption. That coexistence is a function of the theology of the kingdom of God, a topic inseparable from the parables. (Of the eighteen parables in the gospel of Matthew, sixteen of them are explicitly identified as being about the kingdom of God.) The jarring juxtaposition of reasons for despair with reasons for hope is a significant part of what is captured by New Testament parables about the kingdom of God. These parables reinforce the overall gospel message that the kingdom of God is paradoxically both a present reality and a future hope. Jesus's earliest recorded public message was, "The kingdom of God is at hand" (Mark 1:15). Similarly, Jesus told his followers, "The kingdom of God is within you," and he cited his miracles as evidence that "The kingdom of God is come upon you" (Luke 17:21, 11:20). Yet when he taught his disciples to pray, his model prayer included a plea for the kingdom of God to come on earth (Matt. 6:10). This apparent contradiction, it seems, could be best rendered by means of parables. Many of these parables, including those of the sower, the mustard seed, and the leaven, reflect that the growth of the kingdom of God is a mysterious and invisible process, with effects that become visible only after a considerable time. Others, including the wheat and the tares and the dragnet, emphasize that only at the final judgment are the faithful adherents of the kingdom definitively separated from pretenders. Still others, like the ten virgins and the ten talents, suggest that those belonging to the kingdom are in a sense tested according to their faithfulness to that kingdom during a long period of waiting for the kingdom to fully come. According to these parables, the kingdom of God is both here and not here, and that paradox has implications for every aspect of life.

These remarks are the merest sketch of an enormous topic within Christian theology and specifically within discussions of the parables.[21] My basic point – that Jesus's parables of the kingdom of God juxtapose what we may call realist reasons for skepticism or despair with idealist convictions that sustain hope – is more limited and can be sufficiently illustrated by a single example. In the parable of the wheat and the tares, Jesus compares the kingdom of God to a farmer who plants wheat in a field,

> But while men slept, his enemy came and sowed tares among the wheat, and went his way. But when the blade was sprung up, and brought forth fruit, then appeared the tares also. So the servants of the householder came and said unto him, Sir, didst not thou sow good seed in thy field? from whence then hath it tares? He said unto them, An enemy hath done this. The servants said unto him, Wilt thou then that we go and gather them up? But he said, Nay; lest while ye gather up the tares, ye root up also the wheat with them. Let both grow together until the harvest: and in the time of harvest I will say to the reapers, Gather ye together first the tares, and bind them in bundles to burn them: but gather the wheat into my barn. (Matt. 13:25-30)

The surprise, discouragement, and misdirected zeal of the servants in this parable signal various inappropriate responses to the fact that the kingdom of God presently coexists with alien and hostile elements. The farmer, for his part, is neither surprised at his enemy's sabotage nor at a loss as to what to do about it. Confident in the eventual sorting out of the good and bad, he is content to leave both in the field to grow. The farmer's response is of course the privileged one: the disciples are asked to realize that throughout the time in between the planting and the harvest, or between the arrival and the fulfillment of God's kingdom, the good and the bad will be mingled.

The stewardship parables we have already examined share this eschatological import. The parable of the pounds is told specifically to correct the error of those followers of Christ who "thought that the kingdom of God should immediately appear" (Luke 19:11). The closely-related parable of the stewards also speaks directly to the conduct of leaders during the time of Jesus's absence, between the resurrection and the second coming. Victorian cleric Robert Govett's explication of the parable of the stewards, for example, primarily addresses its apocalyptic meaning, noting that the sin of the foolish steward begins with his skepticism about the master's return (38). These parables, then, reflect the paradox of the kingdom of God as both a present reality and a future hope. God's gifts sustain the community in the present, and at Jesus's return the fullness of the kingdom will be given to those who have been faithful (the master will "make him ruler over all he hath") or denied to those who have been unfaithful (the master will "appoint him a portion with the unbelievers"). In other words, the parables place temporal stewardship in the context of cosmic time and ultimate reckoning.

The view of reality suggested here is one that enables the simultaneous apprehension of the world's corruption and the preservation of hope for ultimate redemption. To put it another way, a Christian worldview does not deny the evidence that the world is thoroughly and painfully awry. The perseveration of hope does not require that the good in the world outweigh the bad at any particular moment; in fact, the Christian doctrine of original sin predicts that the bad will, on balance, outweigh the good more often than not. Christian hope can be described as having one's eyes fully open to all that can be seen, while still affirming the reality of that which cannot be seen. As Chesterton says in his discussion of Dickens, "If we are idealists about the other world we can be realists about this world" (194).[22]

From this standpoint, then, discussions about whether the good or bad elements finally prevail in the world of a Dickens novel are beside the point. To read Dickens in this way we need not maintain that Dickens subscribed to the theology of the kingdom of God that I have just outlined, but only that elements of Dickens's narrative patterns – including his cheery resolutions that, however limited they may be, he seems unable to do without – owe something to the pattern and paradoxes of what he famously called "the best book that ever was or will be known in the world."[23]

Dickens himself described his fiction as analogous to the biblical narrative's providential understanding of history. As late as 1859, he wrote to Wilkie Collins, "I think the business of Art is to lay all that ground carefully, but with the care that conceals itself – to shew, by a backward light, what everything has been working to – but only to *suggest*, until fulfillment comes. These are the ways of Providence – of which ways, all Art is but a little imitation."[24] This proleptically suggested fulfillment may fall outside the narrative proper. In discussing providential justice in *Our Mutual Friend*, John R. Reed points out that the narrator's insistence on the imminent demise of the Veneering façade of prosperity – that Mr. Veneering would be bankrupt the next week – should condition the reader's sense of the brevity and insubstantiality of Society's supposed deliverances (*Dickens and Thackeray* 300). Hence "the implied author suggests a pattern of retribution that extends beyond the novel's text and encompasses it. This suggestion is magnified by the use of prolepsis, especially when what is foretold is the *fulfillment of justice beyond the limits of the narrative's action*" (301, emphasis added). As A. E. Dyson writes of Dickens's "view of human virtue": "We live in a world where dynamic virtue exists, and has peculiar attractions and unmistakable authority; but where evil is rampant, and in actual situations may well come off best" (263).[25]

The expectation shown by the (mostly American) critics that Dickens, if he still had any real hope for his society, would have written a triumphalistic book in which the good news somehow shouted down the bad news within the text, may arise from the same distorted understanding of hope and faith that Terry Eagleton attributes to American intellectuals generally. In his recent reflection on *Reason, Faith, and Revolution*, Eagleton insists that the American tendency to "pathological upbeatness ... is by no means to be confused with the virtue of hope" (138). On the contrary, a realism that he describes as Christian – insisting centrally on the inhumanity and evil expressed in Jesus's crucifixion and therefore rejecting what he calls "superstitious" faith in inevitable human progress – makes it possible to live in a socially transformative way even in a blighted world. Eagleton therefore describes Christian faith in terms that could equally well describe Dickens's implied attitude in *Our Mutual Friend*: authentic Christian faith is "the kind of commitment made manifest in a human being at the end of his tether, foundering in darkness, pain, and bewilderment, who nevertheless remains faithful to the promise of a transformative love" (37). In this view, Dickens's work partakes most strongly of a Christian flavor precisely where he gives up on Whiggish "progress," despairing of the potential of programmatic reform to make his society just and merciful, as long as "faithful[ness] to the promise of transformative love" survives. Such faithfulness indeed survives in *Our Mutual Friend* in extravagant acts of self-effacing stewardship in which ordinary capitalistic conduct is startlingly juxtaposed to extraordinary choices to act out of love rather than self-interest. Those choices redescribe human experience, to use Ricoeur's phrase, and they make visible alternatives to the norms of greed and injustice.

Those like Barry Qualls who emphasize the lack of an "apocalyptic pattern" (134) in *Our Mutual Friend* would do well to remember that the gospels, to which Dickens repeatedly affirmed his allegiance until the end of his life, also do not end in an apocalypse. They climax in a resurrection, as does *Our Mutual Friend*. Eugene Wrayburn's and John Harmon's respective symbolic restorations to life, ingeniously contrived within the realist plot, serve to keep alive the hope for the survival and extension of human goodness in the meantime *until* the apocalypse. In particular, Eugene's more unexpected resurrection, combined with his surprising enactment of the rightly-ordered outcomes of both the prodigal son and the stewardship parables, signals his witness to a present though unfulfilled kingdom of harmony and justice. These resurrections, like the faithful stewardship practiced by the Boffins and Harmon, do no more and no less than to "*suggest*" the longed-for restoration of the social body "until fulfillment comes."

# AFTERWORD

Parables are generically tuned to provoke a response, and that is true of the parabolic novels examined here. Yet parables also deny the adequacy of any response we give, individually or collectively. They always have to be read again, and they always discover and rediscover our hidden complacencies, which, like a flock of birds, tend to settle down again on a perch near that from which they have been startled. In what I regard as the most important, culminating lines in Ricoeur's discussion of parable, the philosopher writes that paradox is not merely a language game to be

> lived out in loneliness and impotence. There is paradox ... because the distance of irony and skepticism is excluded, and because paradox disorients only to reorient. What is more ... religious discourse also modifies every expression, be it speculative, practical, ethical, or political. None are privileged, all are affected. ... What I am saying is that the properly religious moment of all discourse, including all political discourse, is the 'still more' that it insinuates everywhere, intensifying every project in the same manner, including the political project. ... Paradox then does not strike *praxis* any less than it does *theoria*, political *praxis* any less than the *praxis* of private morality. It just prevents us from converting religious discourse entirely into political discourse – for the same reason that it forbids its conversion into moral discourse.... (126–127, emphasis in original)

Those who are concerned that the ethical turn in criticism is an ill-advised distraction from political concerns, or that the religious turn in criticism is a step back from political progressivism, operate from a misconception about the nature and function of religious discourses, including fiction in the parabolic tradition. What Ricoeur calls religious discourse, of which parables are exemplary, supplies to both politics and private morality an urgent call to "a quest that cannot be exhausted by any program of action" (126–127). That quest intensifies the pursuit of justice and liberation no less than other individual and collective pursuits of the good. One of the important gifts of parables, then, is their ever-renewed disruption of the systems and conventions by which we insulate our self-regard and self-interests from the full claims of justice. Appreciating how such challenges have been made historically by means of parables in literary history quickens our ability to see and respond to the pressing political and ethical problems of our local and global communities.

At her best, Oliphant's love for her sons caused her to forgive and embrace without illusions or conditions. At his best, Dickens's cudgeling of oppressive institutions and structures drew strength from intuitions of justice and kindness. Yonge's characters, at their best, bear witness to a vision of a transformed life of joyful dignity and humility. None of this is to suggest letting these authors off their shortcomings or blind spots of self-protective paternalism, self-aggrandizing crusading, passive aggression, or what have you. But the parables seem to nurture their most humane imaginations and perhaps their most humane selves as well. As with the canonical parables, so with these novels: to read them well we must be open to be read by them. We, as well as the Victorians, need the animating call to "still more."

# NOTES

## CHAPTER 1

1. See, for example, *Dawning Lights*, 13, 17.
2. A version of this interpretation was a Victorian commonplace: the parable of the prodigal son was frequently described as "the gospel in a parable" and was widely regarded as containing the germ of the gospel message. Nevertheless, such a reading requires, among other things, neglecting the place of the parable in Luke's narrative, where it appears as a reproach against the "Pharisees and scribes" who criticized Jesus for consorting with "publicans and sinners" (Luke 15:1-2).
3. Several guides have aided me in finding my way through a mass of volumes on the subject. I am especially indebted to Kissinger, Champion, and Boadt.
4. See Mark Turner, *The Literary Mind*. More recently, see Michael Burke, "Literature as Parable."
5. Aristotle's definition of *parabole* as an illustrative story, whether historical or fictional, is misleading for most purposes of understanding parable in the West.
6. Stern, *Parables* 9; Jeremias 17-18; Drury, *Parables* 8-20.
7. Many critics view this parable as paradigmatic in the Hebrew Scriptures, including Kermode ("New Ways with Bible Stories") and Thoma. Thoma also points out, however, that unlike Nathan's parable to David, the later rabbinic parables are always addressed to the believing community, not to an individual (30). For a very different reading of this parable, see Schipper 41-56.
8. The parable's conjunction of reversal and self-knowledge corresponds to Aristotle's theory that *peripeteia* and *anagnorisis* (recognition or discovery) are linked: "The finest form of Discovery is one attended by Peripeties" (*Poetics* 11, 1452a33).
9. For more on the parables in the Hebrew Scriptures (as opposed to the later rabbinic parables of the midrash), see Polk and Schipper.

10 The relationship between the Jewish and Christian parable is complicated and contested. The largest body of Jewish parables are the rabbinic parables of the midrash, compiled during the third to the fifth centuries of the Common Era from materials and oral traditions developed beginning before the time of Jesus. Consequently David Stern suggests that the parables of Jesus are perhaps the earliest written record of this tradition of parables ("Jesus's Parables and Rabbinic Literature" 43). Until recently most scholars of Christian parables emphasized the artistic and ideological superiority of Jesus's parables to the rabbinic parables recorded in the midrash (see, for example, Jones 78-9, 240 and Jeremias 10). This bias has been challenged by the more full and systematic study of the midrashic parables and by the increasing emphasis on the importance of the Jewish story and context for the development of early Christianity, including the composition of the gospels (see Flusser; Young; and Stern, *Parables in Midrash*). For an account of these developments, see the essays collected in *Parable and Story in Judaism and Christianity*, especially the essays by Flusser, Thoma, Stern, Milavec, and Boadt.

11 Dan Via helpfully categorizes the parables of Jesus as (1) parables of similitude, (2) the example story, and (3) the true parable, which consists of an invented narrative of particular actions in which the interpretation is not transparent (11–13). In this study I am concerned with the third group of true parables.

12 It has been suggested that Jesus was actually quite close to the Pharisees doctrinally. See Maccoby, *Jesus the Pharisee*.

13 *Quaestiones Evangeliorum* II.19.

14 See Wailes and Kissinger.

15 Dodd is not blind to the difficulties of trying to imagine "such ideas as may have been supposed to have been in the minds of the hearers of Jesus during His ministry" (32), but he overestimates his (or anyone's) ability to negotiate those difficulties.

16 T. R. Wright notes that "the [biblical] text retains an element of indeterminacy of the kind enjoyed more by literary scholars than theologians" (Wright, *Theology and Literature* 78). For more on narrative theology, see McConnell, Loughlin, and Horne. Boadt points to narrative theology as a productive common ground between studies of *meshalim* in the Hebrew Bible and studies of Jesus's parables. For a recent study linking narrative theology to the study of literature, see Knight, *Introduction*.

17 See Frei, *Theology and Narrative*.

18 This narrative theology, as Frei shows, is not a new development of the last quarter of the twentieth century but rather a recovery of the normative theological orientation and ecclesiological and liturgical

experience of Christians from their earliest traceable history to at least the late 1700s. This view of Christianity's historical orientation helps explain why Anglo-American literary studies were so much indebted to biblical exegesis at least until well into the twentieth century. See Suzy Anger, *Victorian Interpretation*, and Stephen Prickett, *Words and the Word*.

19  From another angle Madeline Boucher challenges Dodd's and Jeremias's categorical rejection of allegory as a possible device in a parable. Boucher shows that allegory and parable belong to different categories of rhetoric and are therefore not mutually exclusive. A parable can use allegory just like a parable or a realist novel can use metaphor or any other trope. Drury also challenges the categorical exclusion of allegory ("The Sower").

20  Via 13–25. Via also saw that this severely historical insistence on there being one correct or legitimate point to each parable assumes the irrelevance of aesthetic form to the determination of the theological or moral import of the parable (24).

21  See John Drury, *The Parables in the Gospels*.

22  Funk sees himself in line with Ernst Fuchs, and like Fuchs he formulates his view of parables as language-events along lines supplied by "Heidegger's position that reality is constituted linguistically" (Funk, *Language* 51).

23  Funk attributes to Fuchs this view that the reader's spontaneous emotional reaction to the parable reveals, in effect, which side the reader is already on. Funk himself emphasizes rather the choice that confronts the reader of the parable, who is forced to "choose between two worlds" of conventional reality or a reality reconstituted by grace (*Language* 162).

24  Structuralist readings included the intense but short-lived examination of the parables by members of the Society of Biblical Literature's Parables Seminar in the 1970s. These discussions and debates were published in volumes 1, 2, and 4 of *Semeia* and in the essay collection *Semiology and Parable*. For a generally dim assessment of the results of this structuralist project, see Kissinger 219–220 and Perrin 180–81. Feminist readings include Sallie McFague TeSelle's claim that the parables' real message, contrary to their surface images, is that God is more like a mother than like a father, and more like a liberator than king (*Metaphorical* 21). Elizabeth Dowling's feminist-Foucauldian approach reads the parable of the pounds as "a story about the use and abuse of power" and about "those who suffer adverse consequences when they oppose unjust power structures" (Dowling 1). William Herzog reads the parables as exposés of "the gory details of how oppression served the

interests of a ruling class" (Herzog 3). Mary Ann Tolbert emphasizes the possibility of competing but equally valid interpretations in *Perspectives on the Parables*, including, for example, a Freudian reading in which the parable of the prodigal son is an allegory of the id, ego, and superego (Tolbert 96–114).

25  As Crossan sees it, when the parables were assimilated into the Christian narrative by the early church, they were rendered into toothless example stories. From this conviction arises Crossan's insistence on the dubious practice of categorically eliminating from consideration the gospel settings and frames of the parables on the grounds of their inauthenticity, a practice which Drury compares to reading Dostoevsky's parable of "The Grand Inquisitor" without reference to its place in *The Brothers Karamazov* (Drury 1). For a critique of the view that the historical Jesus must be always and everywhere discontinuous with the early church, see Wilder, *Early Christian Rhetoric* 82; see also *The Bible and the Literary Critic* 127–128. It has also been noted that Crossan's obsession with the historical Jesus is difficult to reconcile with his dismissal of history in favor of linguisticality in every other respect (Brown and Malbon). In this study I do not concern myself with reconstructing the "authentic" or "historical" words of Jesus. When I refer to the words of Jesus, I mean simply the words attributed to Jesus in the earliest and most canonical Christian writings. There is no recovering the words actually spoken by the Galilean rabbi about whom the gospels were written apart from the tradition represented in those gospels. Of course that tradition is diverse, even among the four evangelists, and much more so beyond them. But for my purposes there is sufficient commonality of theme and message in the gospels to perform the readings required here.

26  In my view, the most successful scholar of parables is Amos Wilder, whose long career spanned many of these developments. Among the first to point up the importance of the literary character of the gospels and parables in the 1960s, Wilder was also heard to address the excesses and distortions of Crossan, Hedrick, and others with his characteristically irenic tone in the 1990s.

27  Ricoeur distinguishes between structuralist methodology, which studies how meaning is made through structure, and structuralist ideology, which absolutely privileges the code at the expense of the message ("Biblical Hermeneutics" 65). By engaging the former while rejecting the latter, Ricoeur is able to offer a discussion of the distinctiveness of parables that transcends the limitations of structuralism.

28 Considering that Harrison's aim is to reconcile traditional humanist reading strategies with poststructuralist ones, it is strange that he does not acknowledge any of the work on parables since Jeremias, though his conclusions largely follow those of Ricoeur.
29 Jill Robbins's *Prodigal Son/Elder Brother* explores the dependence of the Christian hermeneutic tradition on this paradigm (which is traced in part to the two brothers of the parable of the prodigal son) on its way to developing a theory of Judaic exegesis on its own terms.
30 For different contrastive readings of Crossan and Ricoeur, see Oldenhage and Poland.
31 In view of the scope of this book, I will limit my discussion here to studies of the relation of literature to the parables of Jesus. For critical studies of literature indebted to Jewish parables, see David Stern, *Parables in Midrash*, especially Chapter 6 on "The Mashal in Hebrew Literature." See also Alan Mintz.
32 Kermode does not say why this is so. I suppose in 1979 it was felt to be self-evident that an objective, scientific (i.e., legitimately scholarly) interpretation of a text could only be undertaken by someone without a prior formation in identification with the text. At a period after the publication of numerous scholarly works exploding not only the myth of "scientific" objectivity, but also the secularization hypothesis, this assumption seems less obvious, to say the least.
33 For a critique that chimes somewhat with mine, see Wilder, *The Bible and the Literary Critic* 12–36.
34 The phrase is Wilder's; TeSelle uses it several times to characterize the effect of parables on the reader (*Speaking* 73, 77).
35 Some notable exceptions include Westbrook and Steiner. David Jasper uses "parable" aptly to refer to the narrative strategy by which Francois Mauriac's *Noeud de Vipères* "judges us by our response" (62).

## CHAPTER 2

1 At the opposite extreme from Crossan lies Charles Hedrick's claim that the parables are all realism, without extravagance (*Parables* 112–16).
2 See also Funk, *Language* 161.
3 But see Shaw's critique of Levine's position as giving too much ground to realism's self-referentiality and maintaining too little consciousness of how realism can be productive of knowledge in and of the world beyond language, though not in a mechanically or transparently referential way (71).

4 Cf. George Levine, who also celebrates the attempt of novels to enable encounters with alterity without simply assimilating the other to oneself (*Realism, Secularism and Ethics* 248ff).
5 This set of Caroline Levine's interlocutors – she particularly highlights Catherine Belsey, D. A. Miller, and Roland Barthes – would seem to fit in the "negative because totalizing" camp in Shaw's schema.
6 This insight bears on my claim in the first chapter that a historical blindness results from insisting that only the latest instantiations of parables are genuinely parabolic, because they disrupt the reigning conventions we most nearly recognize as such. Realism, Caroline Levine reminds us, was once experimental too. Each of the novels I focus on in this study is arguably anti-conventional in some important way.
7 Caroline Levine's discussion of later Victorian novels by George Eliot, Henry James, and Oscar Wilde proceeds to consider how they set aside the liberatory potential of realism to focus on the inherent representationality of all attempts to get at otherness.
8 See Liesbeth Korthals Altes, "Some Dilemmas of an Ethics of Literature." See also Adam Newton, *Narrative Ethics*, esp. 7–27, and Valerie Wainwright, *Ethics and the English Novel from Austen to Forster*, esp. 45–56.
9 In addition to the works of criticism I have been discussing, Brigid Lowe's *Victorian Fiction and the Insights of Sympathy* is a sharp defense of the positive ethical and political potentiality of the realist novel.
10 Larsen, *A People of One Book*. See also Larsen's refutation of the standard Victorian loss-of-faith story in *Crisis of Doubt*.
11 Other key works in this reappraisal of nineteenth-century religion and culture include Colin Jager, *The Book of God*; William McKelvy, *The English Cult of Literature*; Sue Zemka, *Victorian Testaments*; Mark Knight and Thomas Woodman, eds., *Biblical Religion and the Novel*; Morgan and Williams, eds., *Shaping Belief*; J. Russell Perkin, *Theology and the Victorian Novel*; and Gauri Viswanathan, "The Changing Profession." Less recent but still important are Hilary Fraser, *Beauty and Belief*, and David Jasper and T. R. Wright, eds., *The Critical Spirit and the Will to Believe*. Far from offering any naïve myth of a unified "Christian England," these studies emphasize that the ground was contested on all fronts: theological, liturgical, homiletic, and pragmatic, as well as in all the domains touched by religious questions, including politics, commerce, philanthropy, science, and aesthetics. As Larsen has astutely suggested, the high level of rhetoric of religious decline – both in its quantity and tone – is more an index of the strength of the hold of religious thought on the nation than of its weakness (*Crisis* 10).

12  This corresponds with Charles Taylor's understanding of secularism not necessarily as the decline of religious faith, but as a social condition in which religious faith is construed as a matter of choice which could be otherwise (*A Secular Age*).
13  The parable of the rich man and Lazarus follows the principals into the afterlife (Luke 16).
14  See Knight and Woodman, "Introduction," *Biblical Religion and the Novel*: "It would be a mistake, however, to think that the possibility of transcendence can only be expressed in mythic and anti-realistic forms. . . . [T]he biblical sacred is not so much the miraculous in the sense of extraordinary wonders as the natural seen in its ultimate depth" (5).
15  In Rebecca Styler's account, an early Victorian emphasis on Christianity as dogmatic, rationalistic, and otherworldly gave way later in the century to an emphasis on Christianity as poetic, incarnational, and socially embedded. Such a broad thesis, however, can only survive by making generous caveats to counter-examples, since both tendencies are present in most expressions of Christianity.
16  See Richard Horsley, *Jesus and the Powers* and *Covenant Economics*. See also Bruce Longenecker, *Remember the Poor*, esp. 117–125, and Ben Witherington, *Jesus and Money*. See also chapter five of the present study for a discussion of some of Jesus's parables about money. There is a sense in which Jesus and Paul (the latter is the principal focus of Longenecker's study) are secular figures, but only under a use of the word "secular" that includes the possibility that the secular and the religious are interpenetrated, as Christian and Jewish orthodoxy both claim. Levine's use of "secular" here and elsewhere clearly means "not religious," so his implication is that any person or text that "focuses" on money is not genuinely religious.
17  There may well be a Gnostic quality to the "world-hating Calvinism" that Levine uses to oppose to realism's celebration of the material. But however strong the influence of Evangelicalism was, such Calvinism is not an adequate shorthand for characterizing serious Victorian Christianity (much less orthodox Christianity per se), and Dickens's caricatures of it should be seen for the hyperbole they are.
18  See "Gnosticism" by René Braun in *The Oxford Companion to Christian Thought* (268–269) and "Gnosis, Gnosticism" by Peter Nagel in *The Encyclopedia of Christianity* (417–421).
19  The Christology sketched here also enables typological reading, which has been shown to be highly influential on the Victorians (see Landow). Bishop Joseph Butler's classic treatise on *The Analogy of Religion* made the case, decisively for many Victorians, that certain of God's creations were created as they were in order to function

as types, bearing witness to spiritual reality beyond themselves and beyond the material world. In this view, material things enable rather than block access to transcendence.

20  Some work on literary ethics avoids the subject of religion, wanting to separate human goodness from belief in the divine. At other times the connection is indicated but not explored. For example, the essay collection *Theology and Literature: Rethinking Reader Responsibility* includes illuminating treatments of narrative ethics, including essays by Altes and Hurley. But despite the collection's title, none of the essays is much concerned with theology, except possibly that of Nissen. Valerie Wainwright's *Ethics and the English Novel from Austen to Forster* examines how nineteenth-century novels engage in eudaimonistic experiments that follow from and also complicate received moral psychology, but in Wainwright's account religion has no part in that psychology, and even "saintliness" is a wholly humanistic category. David Jasper's *The Study of Literature and Religion* does consider ethics under the rubric of religion, but with implications chiefly for the act of reading only, not for life outside the text. George Levine in *Realism, Secularism and Ethics* explores Victorian thinking about whether and how ethics can be preserved when faith is abandoned. But he is more interested in the disaggregation of the two domains than in their relatedness.

21  It is not that the Victorians could not conceive of an ethics that was not religious; clearly many did. But on the whole they could not think about ethics without reference to religion, or about religion without reference to ethics or morality, even when their aim was to diminish or sever that linkage.

## CHAPTER 3

1  This use of the word parable resembles that of John Coleridge Patteson, Bishop of Melanesia, whose biography Yonge wrote in 1873. Referring to the difficulty of translating Christian concepts using the vocabulary of the indigenous language, Patteson wrote that the parable is the model for elementary Christian instruction that transcends cultural and linguistic differences: "A certain lawyer asked [Jesus] for a definition of his neighbour, but He gave no definition, only He spoke a simple and touching parable. So teach, not a technical word, but an actual thing" (*Life of John Coleridge Patteson* 191).

2  See Dennis, Langbauer, Sandbach-Dahlström, Schaffer ("The Mysterious Magnum Bonum"), and Wheatley.

3  For a particularly vituperative example, see Q. D. Leavis, "Charlotte Yonge."
4  See, for example, "The Author of *Heartsease* and Modern Schools of Fiction;" Coleridge 183; and Bailey 198.
5  On the theologically and philosophically formative aspect of Yonge's relationship with Keble, see Maria Poggi Johnson's "The Reason for What is Right: Practical Wisdom in John Keble and Charlotte Yonge."
6  See Elisabeth Jay's observations about typology as a component of aesthetic theory in *The Heir of Redclyffe*, ("Charlotte Mary Yonge and Tractarian Aesthetics," 55). Also see Rosemary Mitchell, whose discussion of Yonge's *Chantry House* engages questions of historical typology.
7  Virginia Bemis suggests that Yonge's "favored mode of teaching was the parable rather than the sermon," but she does not attempt to apply this claim in any depth to any particular novel (124).
8  This view has begun to change, thanks to recent studies that have complicated the critical picture of Victorian literary antifeminism and of religious literature. See the two collections of relevant studies edited by Tamara Wagner: *Antifeminism and the Victorian Novel: Rereading Nineteenth-Century Women Writers*, particularly the articles on Yonge by Moruzi, Shakinovsky, Juckett, and Schaffer; and the special edition of *Women's Writing* devoted to Yonge (vol. 17.2, Aug 2010). See also Fessler and Thorne-Murphy.
9  See also James Pereiro, *Ethos and the Oxford Movement*, which unpacks the philosophical underpinnings of the Oxford Movement and explores the relationship the movement's early proponents saw between truth and ethics, or right reason and right action.
10  Miller focuses on Newman's take on knowledge of the natural world while mentioning his related take on knowledge of the moral self. Also see Pereiro, who focuses more on Newman's cautions about knowledge of the moral self (111–115).
11  In his *Lectures on Poetry*, Keble claims that the "strong tie of kinship which binds [religion and poetry] together" is "a tone of modest and religious reserve" (481–82). Keble directly applies his remarks only to poetry, not to fiction, but Yonge's clear intention to write realist fiction in the vein of Tractarian aesthetics warrants our extending the application to her novels.
12  See my article on "Realism and Reserve: Charlotte Yonge and Tractarian Aesthetics." Also see Engel.
13  This sermon postdates *Heir* by a number of years, but another sermon by Pusey on the same parable was published as early as 1833, indicating that the subject was on his mind for some time. Yonge was

undoubtedly familiar with Pusey's work from her close association with Keble. Whether or not Pusey had any direct influence on Yonge's conceptualization of Philip (or, for that matter, whether or not the character of Philip had any influence on Pusey's understanding of the Pharisee), it is enough to see that Pusey and Yonge present two very similar versions of a Tractarian understanding of Pharisaism.

14  Yonge was familiar with this book and recommended it in her guide for Sunday-School teachers, *How to Teach the New Testament* (ch. V, I.5).

15  Philip becomes a conventional hypocrite when, after contracting his secret understanding with Laura, he actively persecutes Guy as an untrustworthy spouse for Amy. However, this hypocrisy, while of course mentioned, is passed over lightly by the perceptive characters, such as Charlie, who express Yonge's view that Philip's root sins are self-righteousness and self-complacency. Georgina Battiscome is, as far as I can tell, the only critic Victorian or modern who has identified Philip as a Pharisee in print (Battiscome 77).

16  Yonge's epistolary discussion of the novel's progress with Dyson was particularly copious, no doubt due to the fact that the germ of the story had been conceived by Dyson. Yonge scrupulously credited Dyson throughout her life, even saying that *Heir* was better than the rest of her books because the idea had not been her own (Romanes 63).

17  See Catherine Wells-Cole's discussion of anger as a threat to masculine virtue and to men's assimilation into the domestic sphere of women in several Yonge texts.

18  Paul's self-description in his epistle to the Philippians includes the comments: "as touching the law, a Pharisee; Concerning zeal, persecuting the church; touching the righteousness which is in the law, blameless" (Phil. 3:5-6).

19  On the road to Damascus, Paul was blinded by "a light from heaven;" then he "fell to the ground," and the voice of Jesus accused Paul of "persecuting" him (Acts 9:3-4). Three days after being blinded on the road, Paul met the Christian Ananias who lay hands on Paul: "Immediately there fell from his eyes as it had been scales: and he received his sight forthwith" (Acts 9:18).

## CHAPTER 4

1  For more on this relationship see Jay, *Mrs. Oliphant* 167, 303–4; and M. Williams, *Margaret Oliphant* 122–3.

2  Maggie's death occurred between the writing of part X, ending with Chapter 23, and part XI. Since Oliphant was two parts ahead of the publication schedule, the February and March parts appeared

without interruption following the January death; April's installment was missed, and the novel continued with Chapter 24 in May. Some of the treatment of providential justice I will be examining here, including the use of the prodigal son parable to problematize that justice, was therefore present in the novel before Oliphant's bereavement, showing that Oliphant's abiding questions about why suffering is so unequally distributed on earth did not begin with Maggie's death. Its most pointed expression, however, occurring in the conversation between Gerald and Frank after Gerald's conversion, was written after Maggie's death.

3  A similar circumstance occurs in *The Prodigals and their Inheritance*. Although that novel centers on the faithful daughter, in it too Oliphant emphasizes that the two prodigal sons bring ungentlemanly habits and unfilial dispositions into their late father's home.
4  See the quite similar asides on pp. 98 and 219.
5  Margarete Rubik's work on Oliphant (*Novels*, "Subversion," and "Return") focuses on the coexistence in Oliphant of, on the one hand, traditional themes and a few Victorian prejudices and, on the other hand, a readiness to challenge and subvert many Victorian conventions. However, her discussion of *Who Was Lost and Is Found* somehow misses this tension: she does not notice the critique Oliphant sustains of Mrs. Oglivy or of the parable to which she appeals (*Novels* 199).
6  Quoted in Jay, *Mrs. Oliphant* 147. The direct target of this criticism is Dickens.
7  Consider, for example, Oliphant's reviews of works like Renan's *Life of Jesus* ("The Life of Jesus") and F. D. Maurice's *The Doctrine of Sacrifice* ("Modern Light Literature – Theology").
8  *Autobiography* 52 and 80, "Fancies" 250.
9  In "Modern Light Theology," Oliphant criticizes a strain of modern divinity that, in effect, brings God to the bar "with a real and true desire that the glorious Examinant before them should vindicate His own character according to their idea of it" (74).
10  In the best reading of Oliphant's religion, Elisabeth Jay discusses matters such as Oliphant's church affiliation and clerical friendships alongside her fiction and nonfiction to paint a nuanced picture of Oliphant's religious beliefs and values (*Mrs. Oliphant* 139–91). Rubik's treatment of "the metaphysical world," including the clerical social comedies and the supernatural stories, in her full-length study of *The Novels of Margaret Oliphant* is also well-grounded and nuanced (225–298). Vineta and Robert Colby suggest that "the best of [Oliphant's] religious fiction is pious without being pietistic" (xii). They explore this claim chiefly with reference to the

supernatural fiction, though they gesture towards Oliphant's careful "balance between religion and social comedy" in *The Perpetual Curate* (60). Though monographs and biographies on Oliphant do not ignore religion in their subject, most of the articles produced in the last two or three decades make no reference to religious matters.

11  Some of the studies that focus on these novels include those by Langland, Michie, Milton, O'Mealy ("Mrs. Oliphant" and "Rewriting"), A. Robinson, and Cohen.

12  See Heilmann, A. Sanders, Schaub, Peterson ("Female *Bildungsroman*"), and M. Williams ("Feminist or Anti-feminist?"). For treatments of gender politics that focus on Oliphant's periodical writing, see Scriven and J. Smith.

13  Aside from Joanne Shattock's study of the editorial relationship between John Blackwood and Oliphant, most of the scant critical attention given to *The Perpetual Curate* concerns its treatment of clerical characters. See O'Mealy, "Scenes of Professional Life," and the briefer discussion in Oliver Lovesey. Also see M. Williams, *Margaret Oliphant* 78–81.

14  For example, Schaub makes a strong case for Oliphant's anti-idealism with regard to gender ideology.

15  In *The Novels of Margaret Oliphant*, Rubik qualifies this view of the author's subversiveness by also giving attention to the moral and religious orthodoxy that underlies Oliphant's work. In particular, Rubik is aware that "Although she concentrates on social phenomena in her novels, she does not avoid confronting the central issues of faith" and that "Despite [Oliphant's] keen eye for self-deception and hypocrisy, Oliphant by no means questions or ridicules genuine religious convictions" (227, 232).

16  This overall view of Oliphant's fiction may explain why M. Williams regards the prodigal son subplot in *The Perpetual Curate* as unsuccessful (*Margaret Oliphant* 80).

17  Cf. Lovesey, who regards the Chronicles of Carlingford as religious novels but only in the Trollopean, demythologizing sense (21, 26).

18  Leila Walker suggests that Oliphant "seems to denigrate her own substantive ideas by expressing them in a genre that is not usually afforded much respect. However, it is this denigration itself that allows Oliphant to explore a more nuanced political position than what she expresses in her overtly political essays" (178). I offer essentially the same suggestion about Oliphant's religious thought.

19  Analogously, Schaub points out that Oliphant's irony about gender ideology confuses critics. She argues that Oliphant is indirectly but unambivalently feminist, though her irony makes that difficult to see.

20  Jay elsewhere writes, "[T]he fervency of her desire to believe in a divine final chapter to the human story is constantly challenged by a structure that underlines her accompanying sense of life's random plotlessness" ("Freed by Necessity" 144).
21  In her article on Oliphant's endings, Amy Robinson cautions against the habit of equating conventional ending with conservative politics.
22  The only real controversy concerns the relation of the parable to the doctrine of the atonement. Opponents of substitutionary atonement liked to emphasize that the parable of the prodigal son contains no reference to this doctrine, in that the father does not demand the intervention of one brother in order to forgive the other. See, for example, Frances Power Cobbe's rewriting of the parable to include the atonement (*Broken Lights* 49ff; see 1–2 of the present study). An argument against this view can be found in Trench, who counters that no parable should be regarded as a comprehensive soteriology (409), and in Arnot (443–444).
23  My survey has not of course been exhaustive, but I have looked at most of the most popular and widely-printed nineteenth-century treatments of the parable. Among them are Arnot, Bullock, Ferguson, Guthrie, Hamilton, Trench, and Spurgeon, as well as lesser-known sermons or articles by Maclachlan and Punshon. See also John Reed's discussion of the trope of the prodigal in Victorian literature, especially his comments on the valorization of the prodigal (*Victorian Conventions* 239–249).
24  In her *Blackwood's* article "Sermons," Oliphant praises preachers who communicate a genuine notion of human existential struggle in contrast to those preachers who only offer idealized portraits of ethereal spiritual victors.
25  See Jay's suggestion that "That capacity for pitting the certainties of orthodoxy against the unfathomable mysteries of man's spiritual condition is one of the greatest strengths of Mrs. Oliphant's fiction" (*Mrs. Oliphant* 191).
26  Oliphant wrote of this story that "It has been written not from the head but from the heart" and that "It hurt me to publish anything so personal" (Oliphant and Coghill 429, 430).

## CHAPTER 5

1  Nancy Hill Klenk rightly observes that parable accommodates Dickens's fusion of what she calls "the metaphysical" and "the empirical" or real. She suggests that Dicken's practice of situating the metaphysical within the real means that *Dombey and Son* is

better described as a parable than as a fairy tale. Jennifer Gribble's excellent reading of *Hard Times* argues that the parable of the Good Samaritan "not only provides interpretative clues to the plot and characterisation, setting, and symbolism of *Hard Times*, but ... it underlies its metadiscursive interest in the nature and significance of narrative" (428).

2. Useful studies of Dickens's own religious positions include Walder, A. Sanders, and Wheeler. J. Hillis Miller's study *Charles Dickens: The World of His Novels* also reaches conclusions in this direction. Karl Ashley Smith's *Dickens and the Unreal City*, while largely focused on Dickens's imagery patterns, addresses the imagery's significance in terms of Dickens's religious commitments to a greater extent than I will do here.

3. See also Zemka 117–47.

4. However, both Mundhenk and Jaffe miss the ethical import of Dickens's strategy of *peripeteia*. For Mundhenk, the reader's "awakening" is "primarily ... aesthetic and cognitive" rather than moral. But clearly for Dickens, "exaggerated pride in [one's] ability to perceive and to judge" is a serious moral flaw (49–50). Jaffe shows that Dickens's manipulation of readers' epistemology justifies seeing Dickens as a proto-modernist in his use of the (so-called) omniscient narrator.

5. Gribble rightly notes that Dickens's fiction "shows a more sophisticated understanding of [parables'] qualities and purposes" than is evident from his explicit comments about parables in *Life of Our Lord* (431).

6. See Sadrin and Reed (*Dickens and Thackeray*).

7. My reading here complements rather than argues with Gallagher's and George Levine's discussions of the role of suspended animation or apparent or symbolic death in the right disposition of wealth. Those critics emphasize that it is only through death that money (Gallagher) or knowledge (Levine) can become life-giving in *Our Mutual Friend*. Yet both of them seem uninterested in the fact that the notion of "life" that is privileged by Dickens is ineluctably rooted in the Christian story and the values that derive from it. Recovering that religious investment will help us explain, to return to Gallagher's and Levine's terms, how and why it is that the liminal state of suspended animation protects one from perverted values. The self-effacement that Levine notices in the novel's life-giving characters has a name familiar to Dickens's New Testament moral framework, and that name is stewardship.

8. Yet another stewardship parable, the parable of the unjust steward, is directly invoked in the text but is not as important to the novel's

underlying themes as those discussed. Dickens's famous comment on Shares, beginning, "As is well-known to the wise in their generation, traffic in shares is the one thing to have to do with in this world" (118) borrows the phrase about "the wise in their generation" from this parable in Luke 16. In this famously difficult parable, the master commends the steward's shrewdness in falsifying bills in order to secure his future provision after he loses his job.

9  See Frank Turner's cogent argument that religious and secular duties were by no means separate categories for most Victorians, but rather were thoroughly interpenetrated (*Contesting Cultural Authority* 3–37).
10  See Govett.
11  See Arnot, Michell, Stirling, and Trench.
12  Govett 5.
13  See Michell, Seeley, and Stirling. For an instance of this interpretation being applied to the parable of the wise steward, see Stubbs, "Progress and Poverty" 305–306.
14  We may be tempted to dismiss this as a myth deployed to disguise capitalistic exploitation, but it is just such myths, according to Terry Eagleton in *Reason, Faith, and Revolution,* that enable one to imagine humane alternatives to the status quo. Similarly Harry Shaw insists that "one of the most important possibilities literature opens to us [is] the possibility of a utopian revolt against the insufficiencies of the present" (62).
15  See notices in *The British Quarterly Review* (vol. 59, Apr. 1874, p. 333); *The Wesleyan-Methodist Magazine* (vol. 20, Aug. 1874, p. 727); *The Theological Review* (vol. 13:53, Apr. 1876, 317); *The Literary World* (vol. 9, 3 Apr. 1876, 218).
16  See, for example, Dickens's *Household Words* article about the ragged school upon which Charley Hexam's first school is apparently modeled: Dickens addresses the clergy, saying "between . . . twenty other edifying controversies, a certain large class of minds in the community is gradually being driven out of all religion! Would it be well, do you think, to come out of the controversies for a little while, and be simply Apostolic thus low down!" ("A Sleep to Startle Us" 580).
17  Stanley Friedman's *Dickens's Fiction* discusses the symmetry between Riah and Boffin, including their roles as stewards: both are "generous, long-suffering, honest, and loyal servants of despicable employers" (133).
18  As Efraim Sicher phrases the question, "[W]hich is truer – that Dickens's novels aimed to reform a corrupt society or that they represented society as irredeemably wicked?" (330). Though

Sicher seems to want to get beyond this question, he does not do so, deciding that "Dickens was attacking abuse more than he was proposing change" (331). My reading escapes this short-sighted binary, which seems to say that Dickens was either without hope or hoped in pragmatic, institutional reform, and therefore mistakenly requires Dickens to eschew the metaphysical realm.

19  Also see Kincaid 228.
20  While I will be agreeing with Knoepflmacher's more positive reading of the novel, I disagree that it is based on fairy tale magic. His use of the phrase "sleight of hand" reduces the magic of fairy tales to the illusionism of an enlightened age: we know it's not really magic, but only magic tricks, that we are seeing. This reading takes us even farther than fairy tales from the real otherworldliness that Dickens's resolutions rely upon. See Nancy Hill for another formulation of this contrast between fairy tale and parable in Dickens.
21  C. H. Dodd argued very influentially for reading the parables as expressions of the kingdom of God. Ricoeur similarly sees the kingdom of God as the referent of the parables, albeit a metaphorical referent (126–127). More recently, see Hedrick, "Parable and Kingdom."
22  Dickens is for Chesterton an instance of the "optimistic reformer," who focuses not on the souls being lost, but "on the fact that they are worth saving" (194). This type of reformer is more successful, Chesterton says, because "he keeps alive in the human soul an invincible sense of the thing being worth doing, of the war being worth winning, of the people being worth their deliverance" (195). George Levine similarly writes, "*Our Mutual Friend* depends on Dickens's feeling for the supreme value of life itself" (*Dying to Know* 158).
23  *Letters of Charles Dickens*, vol. 12, 187–88. To Edward Dickens, Sept. 1868.
24  *Letters of Charles Dickens*, vol. 9, 128. To Wilkie Collins, 6 Oct. 1859.
25  Kincaid captures this tension in another way when he describes *Our Mutual Friend* as "preoccupied with the combined torture and hope of purgatory" (228).

# BIBLIOGRAPHY

Altes, Liesbeth Korthals. "Some Dilemmas of an Ethics of Literature." *Theology and Literature: Rethinking Reader Responsibility.* Eds. Gaye Williams Ortiz and Clara A. B. Joseph. New York: Palgrave Macmillan, 2006. 15–31.
Anger, Suzy. *Victorian Interpretation.* Ithaca, NY: Cornell UP, 2005.
Arnold, Edwin T. "Naming, Knowing and Nothingness: McCarthy's Moral Parables." *Perspectives on Cormac McCarthy.* Eds. Edwin T. Arnold and Dianne C. Luce. Jackson, MS: UP of Mississippi, 1999. 45–69.
Arnold, Matthew. *Literature and Dogma: An Essay Towards a Better Apprehension of the Bible.* (1873) Reprinted. London: John Murray, 1924.
Arnot, William. *The Parables of Our Lord.* London: T. Nelson and Sons, 1865.
Auerbach, Erich. "Figura." *Scenes from the Drama of European Literature: Six Essays.* Trans. Ralph Manheim. New York: Meridian Books, 1959. 11–76.
—. *Mimesis: The Representation of Reality in Western Literature.* Trans. Willard R. Trask. 50th Anniversary Ed. Princeton, NJ: Princeton UP, 2003.
"The Author of *Heartsease* and Modern Schools of Fiction." *The Prospective Review* 10 (1854): 460–482.
Bailey, Sarah. "Charlotte Mary Yonge." *Cornhill* 150 (1934): 188–198.
Battiscome, Georgina. *Charlotte Mary Yonge: The Story of an Uneventful Life.* London: Constable P, 1944.
Bemis, Virginia. "Reverent and Reserved: The Sacramental Theology of Charlotte M. Yonge." *Women's Theology in Nineteenth-Century Britain: Transfiguring the Faith of Their Fathers.* Ed. Julie Melnyk. New York: Garland, 1998. 123–132.
Boadt, Lawrence, C. S. P. "Understanding the Mashal and Its Value for the Jewish-Christian Dialogue in Narrative Theology." *Parable and Story in Judaism and Christianity.* Eds. Clemens Thoma and Michael Wyschogrod. New York: Paulist P, 1989. 159–188.

Boucher, Madeleine I. *The Mysterious Parable: A Literary Study*. The Catholic Biblical Quarterly; Monograph Series. Washington: Catholic Biblical Association of America, 1977.

Brown, Frank Burch and Elizabeth Struthers Malbon. "Parabling as a *Via Negativa*: A Critical Review of the Work of John Dominic Crossan." *The Journal of Religion* 64.4 (1984): 530–538.

Budge, Gavin. *Charlotte M. Yonge: Religion, Feminism and Realism in the Victorian Novel*. Oxford: Peter Lang, 2007.

—. "Realism and Typology in Charlotte M. Yonge's *TheHeir of Redclyffe*." *Victorian Literature and Culture* 31 (2003): 193–223.

Bullock, Charles. *The Way Home: Or, the Gospel in the Parable: An Earthly Story with a Heavenly Meaning*. London: Home Words Publishing Office, 1880.

Burke, Michael. "Literature as Parable." *Cognitive Poetics in Practice*. Eds. Joanna Gavins and Gerard Steen. London: Routledge, 2003. 115–128.

Butler, Joseph. *The Analogy of Religion*. (1736) Ed. Ernest C. Mossner. New York: F. Ungar Pub. Co., 1961.

Champion, James. "The Parable as an Ancient and Modern Form." *Literature and Theology* 3.1 (1989): 16–39.

"Charlotte Mary Yonge." *Church Quarterly Review* 57 (1904): 337–360.

Chesterton, G. K. *Charles Dickens*. (1906) London: Methuen & Co., Ltd., 1925.

Cobbe, Frances Power. *Broken Lights: An Inquiry into the Present Condition and Future Prospects of Religious Faith*. London: Trübner & Co., 1864.

—. *Dawning Lights: An Inquiry Concerning the Secular Results of the New Reformation*. London: Williams and Norgate, 1882.

Cohen, Monica. "Maximizing Oliphant: Begging the Question and the Politics of Satire." *Victorian Women Writers and the Woman Question*. Ed. Nicola Diane Thompson. Cambridge: Cambridge UP, 1999.

Colby, Venita. *Yesterday's Woman: Domestic Realism and the Victorian Novel*. Princeton, NJ: Princeton UP, 1974.

— and Robert A. Colby. *The Equivocal Virtue: Mrs. Oliphant and the Victorian Literary Market Place*. Hamden, CN: Archon Books, 1966.

Coleridge, Christabel. *Charlotte Mary Yonge: Her Life and Letters*. London: Macmillan, 1903.

Colledge, Gary. *Dickens, Christianity, and The Life of Our Lord: Humble Veneration, Profound Conviction*. London: Contiuum, 2009.

Colón, Susan. "Realism and Reserve: Charlotte M. Yonge and Tractarian Aesthetics." *Women's Writing* 17 (2010): 221–235.

Crossan, John Dominic. *Cliffs of Fall: Paradox and Polyvalence in the Parables of Jesus*. New York: Seabury P, 1980.

—. *The Dark Interval: Towards a Theology of Story*. Sonoma, CA: Polebridge P, 1988.
—. *In Parables: The Challenge of the Historical Jesus*. New York: Harper & Row, 1973.
—. *The Raid on the Articulate: Comic Eschatology in Jesus and Borges*. New York: Harper & Row, 1976.
Dennis, Barbara. *Charlotte Yonge (1823–1901), Novelist of the Oxford Movement: A Literature of Victorian Culture and Society*. Lewiston, NY: Edwin Mellen P, 1992.
Dickens, Charles. "A Haunted House." *Household Words* 7.174 (1853): 481–483.
—. *Letters of Charles Dickens*. Gen. Eds. Madeline House, Graham Storey, Kathleen Tillotson. 12 Vols. Oxford: Clarendon, 1965–2002.
—. *The Life of Our Lord*. New York: Simon and Schuster, 1934.
—. *Our Mutual Friend*. (1865) Ed. Adrian Poole. London: Penguin, 1997.
—. "A Sleep to Startle Us." *Household Words* 4.103 (1852): 577–580.
—. *Speeches, Letters, and Sayings of Charles Dickens, to which is added a sketch of the author by George Augustus Sala; and Dean Stanley's Sermon*. New York: Harper, 1870.
Dodd, C. H. *The Parables of the Kingdom*. 3rd ed., reprinted. New York: Charles Scribner's Sons, 1956.
Doloff, Steven. "The Prudent Samaritan: Melville's 'Bartleby, the Scrivener' as Parody of Christ's Parable to the Lawyer." *Studies in Short Fiction* 34.3 (1997): 357–361.
Donahue, John R., SJ. *The Gospel in Parable: Metaphor, Narrative, and Theology in the Synoptic Gospels*. Philadelphia, PA: Fortress P, 1988.
Dowling, Elizabeth. *Taking Away the Pound: Women, Theology and the Parable of the Pounds in the Gospel of Luke*. London: Continuum, 2007.
Drury, John. *The Parables in the Gospels: History and Allegory*. New York: Crossroad, 1985.
—. "The Sower, the Vineyard, and the Place of Allegory in the Interpretation of Mark's Parables." *Journal of Theological Studies* n.s. 24.2 (1973): 367–379.
Dyson, A. E. *The Inimitable Dickens: A Reading of the Novels*. London: Macmillan, 1970.
Eagleton, Terry. *Reason, Faith, and Revolution: Reflections on the God Debate*. New Haven, CT: Yale UP, 2009.
Eisenhauer, Robert. *Parables of Disfiguration: Reason and Excess from Romanticism to the Avante-Garde*. New York: Peter Lang, 2005.
Engel, Elliot. "Heir of the Oxford Movement: Charlotte Mary Yonge's *The Heir of Redclyffe*." *Etudes Anglaises: Grande-Bretagne, Etats-Unis* 33 (1980): 132–141.

Fahlbusch, Erwin, et al., eds. *The Encyclopedia of Christianity*. Trans. Geoffrey W. Bromiley. Grand Rapids, MI: Eerdmans Publishing Co., 2001.

Farrar, F. W. "Westminster Sermons: The Rich Fool." *The Quiver* 12.577 (1877): 741–744.

Ferguson, Fergus. *The Parable of the Prodigal Son: A Homiletic Exposition*. London: Hamilton, Adams, & Co., 1873.

Fessler, Audrey. "Feminist Social Reform and Problems with Patriarchy in Yonge's *The Clever Woman of the Family*." *Gender and Victorian Reform*. Ed. Anita Rose. Newcastle upon Tyne, England: Cambridge Scholars, 2008. 46–57.

Flusser, David. "Aesop's Miser and the Parable of the Talents." *Parable and Story in Judaism and Christianity*. Eds. Clemens Thoma and Michael Wyschogrod. New York: Paulist P, 1989. 9–25.

Fraser, Hilary. *Beauty and Belief: Aesthetics and Religion in Victorian Literature*. Cambridge: Cambridge UP, 1986.

Frei, Hans. *The Eclipse of Biblical Narrative*. New Haven, CT: Yale UP, 1974.

—. *Theology and Narrative: Selected Essays*. Eds. George Hunsinger and William Placher. Oxford: Oxford UP, 1993.

Friedman, Stanley. *Dickens's Fiction: Tapestries of Conscience*. New York: AMS Press, 2003.

Fuchs, Ernst. *Studies of the Historical Jesus*. Trans. Andrew Scobie. London: SCM P, 1964.

Funk, Robert. *Jesus as Precursor*. Ed. Edward F. Beutner. Rev. Ed. Sonoma, CA: Polebridge P, 1994.

—. *Language, Hermeneutic, and Word of God: The Problem of Language in the New Testament and Contemporary Theology*. New York: Harper & Row, 1966.

Gallagher, Catherine. *The Body Economic: Life, Death, and Sensation in Political Economy and the Victorian Novel*. Princeton, NJ: Princeton UP, 2006.

Goodlad, Lauren M. E. *Victorian Literature and the Victorian State: Character and Governance in the Victorian Novel*. Baltimore, MD: John Hopkins, 2003.

Govett, Robert. "The Parable of the Talents Explained." *The Prophesy on Olivet, or Matthew XXIV and XXV Expounded*. Norwich, CT: Fletcher and Son, n.d.

Gribble, Jennifer. "Why the Good Samaritan was a Bad Economist: Dickens' Parable for *Hard Times*." *Literature and Theology* 18.4 (2004): 427–441.

Guthrie, Thomas. *The Parables Read in the Light of the Present Day*. London: Alexander Strahan, 1866.

Ham, James Panton. *Parables of Fiction: A Memorial Discourse on Charles Dickens*. London: Trübner & Co., 1870.

Hamilton, James. *The Parable of the Prodigal Son.* London: J. Nisbet and Co., 1867.
Hardy, Barbara. *The Moral Art of Dickens.* London: The Athlone Press, 1970.
Harrison, Bernard. *Inconvenient Fictions: Literature and the Limits of Theory.* New Haven, CT: Yale UP, 1991.
Hastings, Adrian, Alistair Mason and Hugh Pyper, Eds. *The Oxford Companion to Christian Thought.* Oxford: Oxford UP, 2000.
"Heartsease, or the Brother's Wife." *Fraser's* 50 (1854): 489–503.
Hedrick, Charles W. "Parable and Kingdom: A Survey of the Evidence in Mark." *Perspectives in Religious Studies* 27.2 (2000): 179–199.
—. *Parables as Poetic Fictions.* Peabody, MA: Hendrickson, 1994.
Heilmann, Ann. "Mrs. Grundy's Rebellion: Margaret Oliphant between Orthodoxy and the New Woman." *Women's Writing* 6.2 (1999): 215–237.
Herzog, William. *Parables as Subversive Speech: Jesus as Pedagogue of the Oppressed.* Louisville, KY: Westminster John Knox P, 1994.
Hill, Nancy Klenk. "*Dombey and Son*: Parable for the Age." *Dickens Quarterly* 8.4 (1991): 169–177.
Hornbeck, Bert. *"Noah's Arkitecture": A Study of Dickens's Mythology.* Athens, OH: Ohio UP, 1972.
Horne, Brian. "Theology in the Narrative Mode." *Companion Encyclopedia of Theology.* Eds. Leslie Houlden and Peter Byrne. London: Routledge, 1995.
Horsley, Richard A. *Covenant Economics: A Biblical Vision of Justice for All.* Louisville, KY: Westminster John Knox P, 2009.
—. *Jesus and the Powers: Conflict, Covenant, and the Hope of the Poor.* Minneapolis, MN: Fortress P, 2011.
Hurley, Robert J. "The Ethics of Biblical Interpretation: Rhetorizing the Foundations." *Theology and Literature: Rethinking Reader Responsibility.* Eds. Gaye Williams Ortiz and Clara A. B. Joseph. New York: Palgrave Macmillan, 2006. 45–62.
Jaffe, Audrey. *Vanishing Points: Dickens, Narrative, and the Subject of Omniscience.* Berkeley, CA: U of California P, 1991.
Jager, Colin. *The Book of God: Secularization and Design in the Romantic Era.* Philadelphia, PA: U of Pennsylvania P, 2007.
Jasper, David. *The Study of Literature and Religion: An Introduction.* Minneapolis, MN: Fortress P, 1989.
Jay, Elisabeth. "Charlotte Mary Yonge and Tractarian Aesthetics." *Victorian Poetry* 44.1 (2006): 43–59.
—. "Freed by Necessity, Trapped by the Market: The Editing of Oliphant's *Autobiography*." *Margaret Oliphant: Critical Essays on a Gentle Subversive.* Ed. D. J. Trela. Selinsgrove, PA: Susquehanna UP, 1995. 135–146.

—. *Mrs. Oliphant: "A Fiction To Herself": A Literary Life*. Oxford: Clarendon P, 1995.
Jeffrey, David Lyle. *People of the Book: Christian Identity and Literary Culture*. Grand Rapids, MI: Eerdmans, 1996.
Jeremias, Joachim. *The Parables of Jesus*. Trans. S. H. Hooke. London: SCM P, 1954.
Johnson, Maria Poggi. "The Reason for What is Right: Practical Wisdom in John Keble and Charlotte Yonge." *Literature and Theology* 20 (2006): 379–393.
Jones, Geraint Vaughan. *The Art and Truth of the Parables: A Study in their Literary Form and Modern Interpretation*. London: SPCK, 1964.
Juckett, Elizabeth C. "Cross-Gendering the Underwoods: Christian Subjection in Charlotte Yonge's *The Pillars of the House*." *Antifeminism and the Victorian Novel: Rereading Nineteenth-Century Women Writers*. Ed. Tamara S. Wagner. Amherst, NY: Cambria, 2009. 117–136.
Jülicher, D. Adolf. *Die Gleichnisreden Jesu*. Freiburg I. B.: J. C. B. Mohr, 1899.
Keble, John. "Lecture XL." *Lectures on Poetry*. Trans. Edward Francis. *Aesthetics and Religion in Nineteenth-Century Britain*. Vol. 2. Ed. Gavin Budge. Bristol: Thoemmes P, 2003.
Kermode, Frank. *The Genesis of Secrecy: On the Interpretation of Narrative*. The Charles Eliot Norton Lectures, 1977–78. Cambridge, MA: Harvard UP, 1979.
—. "New Ways with Bible Stories." *Parable and Story in Judaism and Christianity*. Eds. Clemens Thoma and Michael Wyschogrod. New York: Paulist P, 1989. 121–135.
Kincaid, James. *Dickens and the Rhetoric of Laughter*. Oxford: Oxford UP, 1971.
Kissinger, Warren S. *The Parables of Jesus: A History of Interpretation and Bibliography*. Metuchen, NJ: Scarecrow P, 1979.
Knight, Mark. *An Introduction to Religion and Literature*. London: Continuum, 2009.
— and Emma Mason. *Nineteenth-Century Religion and Literature: An Introduction*. Oxford: Oxford UP, 2006.
—. and Thomas Woodman, Eds. *Biblical Religion and the Novel, 1700–2000*. Aldershot, UK: Ashgate, 2006.
Knoepflmacher, U. C. *Laughter and Despair: Readings in Ten Novels of the Victorian Era*. Berkeley, CA: U of California P, 1971.
Kucich, John. "Dickens' Fantastic Rhetoric: The Semantics of Reality and Unreality in *Our Mutual Friend*." *Dickens Studies Annual* 14 (1985): 167–189.
Landow, George P. *Victorian Types, Victorian Shadows: Biblical Typology in Victorian Literature, Art and Thought*. Boston, MA: Routledge & Kegan Paul, 1980.

Langbauer, Laurie. *Novels of Everyday Life: The Series in English Fiction, 1850–1930*. Ithaca, NY: Cornell UP, 1999.
Langland, Elizabeth. "Inventing Reality: The Ideological Commitments of George Eliot's *Middlemarch*." *Narrative* 2.2 (1994): 87–111.
Larsen, Timothy. *A People of One Book: The Bible and the Victorians*. Oxford: Oxford UP, 2011.
—. *Crisis of Doubt: Honest Faith in Nineteenth-Century England*. Oxford: Oxford UP, 2006.
Larson, Janet. *Dickens and the Broken Scripture*. Athens, GA: U of George P, 1985.
Leavis, Q. D. "Charlotte Yonge and 'Christian Discrimination.'" *Scrutiny* 12 (1944): 152–160.
Levine, Caroline. *The Serious Pleasures of Suspense: Victorian Realism and Narrative Doubt*. Charlottesville: U of Virginia P, 2003.
Levine, George. *Dying to Know: Scientific Epistemology and Narrative in Victorian England*. Chicago, IL: U of Chicago P, 2002.
—. *Realism, Ethics, and Secularism: Essays on Victorian Literature and Science*. Cambridge: Cambridge UP, 2008.
—. *The Realistic Imagination: English Fiction from Frankenstein to Lady Chatterley*. Chicago, IL: U of Chicago P, 1981.
Longenecker, Bruce. *Remember the Poor: Paul, Poverty, and the Greco-Roman World*. Grand Rapids, MI: William B. Eerdmans, 2010.
Loughlin, Gerard. *Telling God's Story: Bible, Church, and Narrative Theology*. Cambridge: Cambridge UP, 1996.
Lovesey, Oliver. "Victorian Sisterhoods and Female Religious Vocation in Margaret Oliphant's Chronicles of Carlingford." *Victorian Newsletter* 106 (2004): 21–27.
Lowe, Brigid. *Victorian Fiction and the Insights of Sympathy: An Alternative to the Hermeneutics of Suspicion*. London: Anthem P, 2007.
Lukács, Georg. *The Theory of the Novel*. (1920) Trans. Anna Bostock. Cambridge, MA: The MIT P, 1971.
Maccoby, Hyam. *Jesus the Pharisee*. London: SCM P, 2003.
Maclachlan, Mrs. *Notes on the Parables According to Literal and Futurist Principles of Interpretation*. Edinburgh: Blackwood and Sons, 1873.
McConnell, Frank, ed. *The Bible and the Narrative Tradition*. Oxford: Oxford UP, 1986.
McFague, Sallie. *Metaphorical Theology: Models of God in Religious Language*. Philadelphia, PA: Fortress P, 1982.
McFague TeSelle, Sallie. *Speaking in Parables: A Study in Metaphor and Theology*. Philadelphia. PA: Fortress P, 1975.
McKelvy, William R. *The English Cult of Literature: Devoted Readers 1774–1880*. Charlottesville, VA: U of Virginia P, 2007.

Michell, Richard. "A Sermon on the Parable of the Unjust Steward." *Miscellaneous Sermons*. London: C. J. Barrington, 1823.

Michie, Elsie B. "Dressing Up: Hardy's *Tess of the D'Urbervilles* and Oliphant's *Phoebe Junior*." *Victorian Literature and Culture* 30.1 (2002): 305–323.

Milavec, Aaron A. "A Fresh Analysis of the Parable of the Wicked Husbandmen in the Light of Jewish-Christian Dialogue." *Parable and Story in Judaism and Christianity*. Eds. Clemens Thoma and Michael Wyschogrod. New York: Paulist P, 1989. 81–117.

Miller, Andrew H. *The Burdens of Perfection: On Ethics and Reading in Nineteenth-Century British Literature*. Ithaca, NY: Cornell UP, 2008.

Miller, J. Hillis. *Charles Dickens: The World of His Novels*. Midland Book edition. Bloomington, IN: Indiana UP, 1969.

—. *The Form of Victorian Fiction: Thackeray, Dickens, Trollope, George Eliot, Meredith, and Hardy*. South Bend, IN: Notre Dame UP, 1968.

—. "Parable and Performative in the Gospels and in Modern Literature." *Tropes, Parables, Performatives: Essays on Twentieth-Century Literature*. Durham, NC: Duke UP, 1991. 135–150.

Mills, Kevin. *The Prodigal Sign: A Parable of Criticism*. Brighton: Sussex Academic P, 2010.

Milton, Heather. "The Female Confessor: Confession and Shifting Domains of Discourse in Margaret Oliphant's *Salem Chapel*." *Antifeminism and the Victorian Novel: Rereading Nineteenth-Century Women Writers*. Ed. Tamara S. Wagner. Amherst, NY: Cambria, 2009. 197–216.

Mintz, Alan. "Modern Hebrew Literature as a Source for Jewish Theology: Repositioning the Question." *Parable and Story in Judaism and Christianity*. Eds. Clemens Thoma and Michael Wyschogrod. New York: Paulist P, 1989. 237–251.

"Miss Yonge's Novels." *Christian Remembrancer* 26 (1853): 33–63.

"Miss Yonge's Novels." *North American Review* 80 (1855): 439–459.

Mitchell, Rosemary. "Charlotte M. Yonge: Reading, Writing, and Recycling Historical Fiction in the Nineteenth Century." *Nineteenth-Century Contexts* 31.1 (2009): 31–43.

Morgan, Victoria and Clare Williams, Eds. *Shaping Belief: Culture, Politics and Religion in Nineteenth-Century Writing*. Liverpool: Liverpool UP, 2008.

Moruzi, Kristine. "'The Inferiority of Women': Complicating Charlotte Yonge's Perception of Girlhood in *The Monthly Packet*." *Antifeminism and the Victorian Novel: Rereading Nineteenth-Century Women Writers*. Ed. Tamara S. Wagner. Amherst, NY: Cambria: 2009. 57–75.

Mundhenk, Rosemary. "The Education of the Reader in *Our Mutual Friend*." *Nineteenth-Century Fiction* 34.1 (1979): 41–58.

Naveh, Gila Safran. *Biblical Parables and Their Modern Recreations: From "Apples of Gold in Silver Setting" to "Imperial Messages."* Albany, NY: State U of New York P, 2000.
Newey, Vincent. *The Scriptures of Charles Dickens: Novels of Ideology, Novels of the Self.* Aldershot: Ashgate, 2004.
Newman, John Henry. *Parochial and Plain Sermons.* San Francisco, CA: Ignatius, 1987.
Newton, Adam Zachary. *Narrative Ethics.* Cambridge, MA: Harvard University Press, 1995.
Nissen, Johannes. "Bible and Ethics: Moral Formation and Analogical Imagination." *Theology and Literature: Rethinking Reader Responsibility.* Eds. Gaye Williams Ortiz and Clara A. B. Joseph. New York: Palgrave Macmillan, 2006. 81–100.
Nord, Deborah Epstein. "Dickens's 'Jewish Question': Pariah Capitalism and the Way Out." *Victorian Literature and Culture* 39 (2011): 27–45.
Oldenhage, Tania. *Parables for Our Time: Rereading New Testament Scholarship after the Holocaust.* Oxford: Oxford UP, 2002.
Oliphant, Margaret. *Autobiography.* Ed. Elisabeth Jay. Oxford: Oxford UP, 1990.
—. "The Fancies of a Believer." *Blackwood's Edinburgh Magazine* 157 (1895): 237–255.
—. "The Life of Jesus." *Blackwood's Edinburgh Magazine* 96 (1864): 417–431.
—. "Modern Light Literature—Theology." *Blackwood's Edinburgh Magazine* 78 (1855): 72–86.
—. "The Open Door." (1882) *A Beleaguered City and Other Tales of the Seen and the Unseen.* Ed. Jenni Calder. Canongate Classics. Edinburgh: Canongate Books Ltd., 2000. 171–210.
—. *The Perpetual Curate.* (1864) Ed. Penelope Fitzgerald. Virago Classics. New York: Penguin, 1987.
—. "Sermons." *Blackwood's Edinburgh Magazine* 84 (1858): 728–742.
—. *Who Was Lost and Is Found.* Edinburgh: William Blackwood and Sons, 1894.
Oliphant, Margaret and Mrs. Harry Coghill. *The Autobiography and Letters of Mrs. M. O. W. Oliphant, Arranged and Edited by Mrs. Harry Coghill.* Edinburgh: William Blackwood and Sons, 1899.
O'Mealy, Joseph H. "Mrs. Oliphant, *Miss Marjoribanks*, and the Victorian Canon." *The New Nineteenth Century: Feminist Readings of Underread Victorian Fiction.* Eds. Barbara Leah Harman and Susan Meyer. New York: Garland, 1996. 63–76.
—. "Rewriting Trollope and Yonge: Mrs. Oliphant's *Phoebe Junior* and the Realism Wars." *Texas Studies in Literature and Language* 39.2 (1997): 125–149.

—. "Scenes of Professional Life: Mrs. Oliphant and the New Victorian Clergyman." *Studies in the Novel* 23.2 (1991): 245–261.

Parris, David. "Imitating the Parables: Allegory, Narrative and the Role of Mimesis." *Journal for the Study of the New Testament* 25.1 (2002): 33–53.

Patte, Daniel, ed. *Semiology and Parables: Exploration of the Possibilities Offered by Structuralism for Exegesis*. Pittsburgh, PA: Pickwick P, 1976.

Pereiro, James. *Ethos and the Oxford Movement: At the Heart of Tractarianism*. Oxford: Oxford UP, 2008.

Perkin, J. Russell. *Theology and the Victorian Novel*. Montreal: McGill-Queen's UP, 2009.

Perrin, Norman. *Jesus and the Language of the Kingdom*. Philadelphia, PA: Fortress P, 1976.

Peterson, Linda H. "The Female Bildungsroman: Tradition and Revision in Oliphant's Fiction." *Margaret Oliphant: Critical Essays on a Gentle Subversive*, Ed. D. J. Trela. Selinsgrove, PA: Susquehanna UP, 1995. 66–89.

Poland, Lynn. *Literary Criticism and Biblical Hermeneutics: A Critique of Formalist Approaches*. AAR Academy Series 48. Chico, CA: Scholars P, 1985.

Polk, Timothy. "Paradigms, Parables, and *Měšālim*: On Reading the *māšāl* in Scripture." *CBQ* 45 (1983): 564–583.

Poovey, Mary. *Making a Social Body: British Cultural Formation, 1830–1864*. Chicago, IL: U of Chicago P, 1995.

Prickett, Stephen. *Words and the Word: Language, Poetics, and Biblical Interpretation*. Cambridge: Cambridge UP, 1988.

Punshon, W. Morley. *The Prodigal Son: Four Discourses*. Boston: Roberts Brothers, 1868.

Pusey, E. B. "Our Pharisaism: A sermon preached at St. Paul's, Knightsbridge, on Ash Wednesday, 1868." Plymouth, MA: Devonport Society, 1868.

Qualls, Barry V. *The Secular Pilgrims of Victorian Fiction: The Novel as Book of Life*. Cambridge: Cambridge UP, 1982.

Reed, John R. *Dickens and Thackeray: Punishment and Forgiveness*. Athens, OH: Ohio UP, 1995.

—. *Victorian Conventions*. Athens, OH: Ohio UP, 1975.

Ricoeur, Paul. "Biblical Hermeneutics." *Semeia* 4 (1975): 29–148.

Riggs, Mike. "Parables against Religion: The Modern Miracle of Humanity in O'Neill's Dynamo Cycle." *Journal of American Drama and Theatre* 12.3 (2000): 14–26.

Robbins, Jill. *Prodigal Son/Elder Brother: Interpretation and Alterity in Augustine, Petrarch, Kafka, Levinas*. Chicago, IL: U of Chicago P, 1991.

Robinson, Amy J. "An 'Original and Unlooked-For Ending'? Irony, the Marriage Plot, and the Antifeminism Debate in Oliphant's *Miss Marjoribanks.*" *Antifeminism and the Victorian Novel: Rereading Nineteenth-Century Women Writers.* Ed. Tamara S. Wagner. Amherst, NY: Cambria, 2009. 159–176.

Romanes, Ethel. *Charlotte Mary Yonge: An Appreciation.* London: A. R. Mowbray. 1908.

Rubik, Margarete. *The Novels of Margaret Oliphant: A Subversive View of Traditional Themes.* Writing About Women: Feminist Literary Studies. New York: Peter Lang, 1994.

—. "The Return of the Convict in Mrs. Oliphant's *The Son of His Father.*" *A Yearbook of Studies in English Language and Literature 1985/86.* Ed. Otto Rauchbauer. Vienna: Braumüller, 1986. 201–215.

—. "The Subversion of Literary Clichés in Oliphant's Fiction." *Margaret Oliphant: Critical Essays on a Gentle Subversive.* Ed. D. J. Trela. Selinsgrove, PA: Susquehanna UP, 1995. 49–65.

Sadrin, Anny. *Parentage and Inheritance in the Novels of Charles Dickens.* Cambridge: Cambridge UP, 1994.

Sandbach-Dahlström, Catherine. *Be Good Sweet Maid: Charlotte Yonge's Domestic Fiction: A Study in Dogmatic Purpose and Fictional Form.* Stockholm, Sweden: University of Stockholm, 1984.

Sanders, Andrew. *Charles Dickens: Resurrectionist.* New York: St. Martin's P, 1982.

Sanders, Valerie. *Eve's Renegades: Victorian Anti-Feminist Women Novelists.* New York: St. Martins P, 1996.

Schaffer, Talia. "Maiden Pairs: The Sororal Romance in *The Clever Woman of the Family.*" *Antifeminism and the Victorian Novel: Rereading Nineteenth-Century Women Writers.* Ed. Tamara S. Wagner. Amherst, NY: Cambria: 2009. 97–115.

—. "The Mysterious Magnum Bonum: Fighting to Read Charlotte Yonge." *Nineteenth-Century Literature* 55 (2000): 244–275.

Schaub, Melissa. "Queen of the Air or Constitutional Monarch?: Idealism, Irony, and Narrative Power in *Miss Marjoribanks.*" *Nineteenth-Century Literature* 55.2 (2000): 195–225.

Schipper, Jeremy. *Parables and Conflict in the Hebrew Bible.* Cambridge: Cambridge UP, 2009.

Scriven, Anne M. "Margaret Oliphant's 'Marriage' to Maga." *Scottish Studies Review* 8.1 (2007): 27–36.

Seeley, Mary. *The Kingdom and the People, or the Parables of Our Lord Jesus Christ Explained and Illustrated.* London: Religious Tract Society, 1879.

Shakinovsky, Lynn. "Domestic History and the Idea of the Nation in Charlotte Yonge's *The Heir of Redclyffe.*" *Antifeminism and the*

*Victorian Novel: Rereading Nineteenth-Century Women Writers.* Ed. Tamara S. Wagner. Amherst, NY: Cambria: 2009. 77–96.

Shattock, Joanne. "The Making of a Novelist: Oliphant and John Blackwood at Work on *The Perpetual Curate.*" *Margaret Oliphant: Critical Essays on a Gentle Subversive.* Ed. D. J. Trela. Selinsgrove, PA: Susquehanna UP, 1995. 113–123.

Shaw, Harry. *Narrating Reality: Austen, Scott, Eliot.* Ithaca, NY: Cornell UP, 2004.

Shively, Steven B. "*My Ántonia* and the Parables of Sacrifice." *Literature and Belief* 22 (2002): 51–62.

Sicher, Efraim. *Rereading the City/Rereading Dickens: Representation, The Novel, and Urban Realism.* New York: AMS Press, 2003.

Smith, Julianne. "Private Practice: Thomas De Quincey, Margaret Oliphant, and the Construction of Women's Rhetoric in the Victorian Periodical Press." *Rhetoric Review* 23.1 (2004): 40–56.

Smith, Karl Ashley. *Dickens and the Unreal City: Searching for Spiritual Significance in Nineteenth-Century London.* New York: Palgrave, 2008.

Spurgeon, Charles. *Twelve Sermons on the Prodigal Son and Other Texts in Luke XV.* Grand Rapids, MI: Baker Book House, 1976.

Stanley, Arthur Penrhyn. "Sermon." *Speeches, Letters, and Sayings of Charles Dickens, to which is added a sketch of the author by George Augustus Sala; and Dean Stanley's Sermon.* New York: Harper, 1870. 144–147.

Steiner, Lina. "Pushkin's Parable of the Prodigal Daughter: The Evolution of the Prose Tale from Aestheticism to Historicism." *Comparative Literature* 56.2 (2004): 130–46.

Stern, David. "Jesus' Parables from the Perspective of Rabbinic Literature: The Example of the Wicked Husbandmen." *Parable and Story in Judaism and Christianity.* Eds. Clemens Thoma and Michael Wyschogrod. New York: Paulist P, 1989. 42–80.

—. *Parables in Midrash: Narrative and Exegesis in Rabbinic Literature.* Cambridge: Harvard UP, 1991.

Stirling, James. *The Stewardship of Life, or Studies on the Parable of the Talents.* London: Hodder and Stoughton, 1873.

Stubbs, Charles W. "Progress and Poverty: A Sermon Preached before the University of Oxford." *Good Words* 24 (1883): 302–308.

Styler, Rebecca. *LiteraryTheology by Women Writers of the Nineteenth Century.* Farnham, UK: Ashgate, 2010.

Taylor, Charles. *A Secular Age.* Cambridge: Harvard UP, 2007.

Thoma, Clemens. "Literary and Theological Aspects of the Rabbinic Parables." *Parable and Story in Judaism and Christianity.* Eds. Clemens Thoma and Michael Wyschogrod. New York: Paulist P, 1989. 26–41.

Thompson, Nicola Diane. *Reviewing Sex: Gender and the Reception of Victorian Novels.* New York: Macmillan, 1996.

Thorne-Murphy, Leslee. "The Charity Bazaar and Women's Professionalization in Charlotte Mary Yonge's *The Daisy Chain.*" *Studies in English Literature* 47 (2007): 881–99.

Tolbert, Mary Ann. *Perspectives on the Parables: An Approach to Multiple Interpretations.* Philadelphia, PA: Fortress, 1979.

Trench, Richard Chenevix. *Notes on the Parables of Our Lord.* (1841) London: Kegan Paul, 1898.

Turner, Frank. *Contesting Cultural Authority: Essays in Victorian Intellectual Life.* Cambridge: Cambridge UP, 1993.

Turner, Mark. *The Literary Mind.* New York: Oxford UP, 1996.

Via, Dan O. *The Parables: Their Literary and Existential Dimension.* Philadelphia, PA: Fortress P, 1967.

Viswanathan, Gauri. "The Changing Profession: Secularism in the Framework of Heterodoxy." *PMLA* 123.2 (2008): 466–76.

Wagner, Tamara S. "Marriage Plots and 'Matters of More Importance': Sensationalising Self-Sacrifice in Victorian Domestic Fiction." *Antifeminism and the Victorian Novel: Rereading Nineteenth-Century Women Writers.* Ed. Tamara S. Wagner. Amherst, NY: Cambria, 2009. 137–158.

Wailes, Stephen L. *Medieval Allegories of Jesus' Parables.* Berkeley, CA: U of California P, 1987.

Wainwright, Valerie. *Ethics and the English Novel from Austen to Forster.* Aldershot, England: Ashgate, 2007.

Walder, Dennis. *Dickens and Religion.* London: George Allen and Unwin, 1981.

Walker, Leila. "Ghosts in the House: Margaret Oliphant's Uncanny Response to Feminist Success." *Antifeminism and the Victorian Novel: Rereading Nineteenth-Century Women Writers.* Ed. Tamara S. Wagner. Amherst, NY: Cambria. 177–195.

Watt, Ian. *The Rise of the Novel: Studies in Defoe, Richardson, and Fielding.* London: Chatto and Windus, 1974.

Wells-Cole, Catherine. "Angry Yonge Men: Anger and Masculinity in the Novels of Charlotte M. Yonge." *Masculinity and Spirituality in Victorian Culture.* Eds. Andrew Bradstock et al. Basingstoke, England: Macmillan, 2000. 71–84.

Westbrook, Deanne. "Wordsworth's Prodigal Son: 'Michael' as Parable and as Metaparable." *Wordsworth Circle* 28.2 (1997): 109–119.

Wheatley, Kim. "Death and Domestication in Charlotte M. Yonge's *The Clever Woman of the Family.*" *SEL* 36 (1996): 895–915.

Wheeler, Michael. *Death and the Future Life in Victorian Literature and Theology.* Cambridge: Cambridge UP, 1990.

Wilder, Amos. *The Bible and the Literary Critic.* Minneapolis, MN: Fortress, 1991.
—. *Early Christian Rhetoric: The Language of the Gospel.* Cambridge: Harvard UP, 1971.
Williams, Isaac. "On Reserve in Communicating Religious Knowledge." Tract 80. *Tracts for the Times.* Vol. 4. London: J. G. F. & J. Rivington, 1840.
Williams, Merryn. "Feminist or Antifeminist? Oliphant and the Woman Question." *Margaret Oliphant: Critical Essays on a Gentle Subversive.* Ed. D. J. Trela. Selinsgrove, PA: Susquehanna UP, 1995. 165–180.
—. *Margaret Oliphant: A Critical Biography.* New York: St. Martin's P, 1986.
Witherington, Ben. *Jesus and Money.* Grand Rapids, MI: Brazos P, 2010.
Wolff, Robert Lee. *Gains and Losses: Novels of Faith and Doubt in Victorian England.* New York: Garland, 1977.
Wright, T. R. *Theology and Literature.* Oxford: Basil Blackwell, 1988.
— and David Jasper, Eds. *The Critical Spirit and the Will to Believe: Essays in Nineteenth-Century Literature and Religion.* New York: St. Martin's P, 1989.
Yonge, Charlotte M. *The Clever Woman of the Family.* (1865) Virago Modern Classics. London: Penguin, 1985.
—. *The Daisy Chain, or Aspirations: A Family Chronicle.* (1856). Virago Modern Classics. London: Penguin, 1988.
—. *Heartsease, or The Brother's Wife.* (1854) London: Macmillan and Co., 1908.
—. *The Heir of Redclyffe.* (1853) Oxford: Oxford UP, 1997.
—. *How To Teach the New Testament.* New York: James Pott, 1882.
—. *Life of John Coleridge Patteson: Missionary Bishop of the Melanesian Islands.* London: Macmillan, 1874.
—. *Musings Over the "Christian Year" and "Lyra Innocentium."* 2nd ed. Oxford and London: James Parker and Co., 1872.
—. "The Price of Blood." *More Bywords.* London: Macmillan, 1890.
Young, Brad. *Jesus and His Jewish Parables.* New York: Paulist P, 1984.
Zemka, Sue. *Victorian Testaments: The Bible, Christology, and Literary Authority in Early-Nineteenth-Century British Culture.* Stanford: Stanford UP, 1997.

# INDEX

affect  31, 52, 76, 91, 121
allegory  7, 20, 43, 125n. 19, 126n. 24
  *see also* parables (allegorical exegesis)
Altes, Liesbeth Korthals  128n. 8, 130n. 20
analogy  4–5, 88, 129n. 19
  *see also* typology
Anger, Suzy  125n. 18
antifeminism  131n. 8
Aristotle  5, 123n. 5, 123n. 8
Arnold, Edwin  19
Arnold, Matthew  37
Arnot, William  106, 108, 135n. 23, 137n. 11
associationism  46
atonement  1–2, 135n. 22
Auerbach, Erich  36–7
Augustine  7–8

Bailey, Sarah  131n. 4
Battiscome, Georgina  132n. 15
Bemis, Virginia  131n. 7
Boadt, Lawrence  123n. 3, 124n. 10, 124n. 16
Borges, Juan Luis  16–17, 25
Boucher, Madeleine  125n. 19
Budge, Gavin  43, 45
Bullock, Charles  135n. 23
Burke, Michael  123n. 4
Butler, Joseph  129n. 19

Champion, James  123n. 3
Chesterton, G. K.  94, 117, 138n. 22
Cobbe, Frances Power  1–2, 31, 135n. 22
Cohen, Monica  134n. 11
Colby, Robert  133n. 10
Colby, Venita  59, 133n. 10
Coleridge, Christabel  53, 58, 131n. 4
Colledge, Gary  96
conversion  15, 18, 51, 58, 60, 83, 114, 121, 133n. 2
Crossan, John Dominic  11–12, 14–15, 17–19, 24–6, 65, 126n. 25

Dennis, Barbara  59, 130n. 2
Dickens, Charles  3, 20, 38, 51, 93–119, 122, 133n. 6
  moral views  106
  religious views  40, 64, 95–6, 106, 136n. 2
  works,
    *Bleak House*  95–6, 114
    *Household Words*  137n. 16
    *Life of Our Lord*  136n. 5
    *Little Dorrit*  96
    *Oliver Twist*  95
    *Our Mutual Friend*  39, 94, 97–119, 136n. 7

didacticism 11–12, 15, 30, 42–3, 61
Dodd, C. H. 6, 8, 10–11, 124n. 15, 125n. 19, 138n. 21
Doloff, Steven 19
Donahue, John 78
Dostoevsky, Fyodor 17, 126n. 25
Dowling, Elizabeth 125n. 24
Drury, John 123n. 6, 125n. 19, 125n. 21, 126n. 25
Dyson, A. E. 118

Eagleton, Terry 36, 118, 137n. 14
Eisenhauer, Robert 20
Engel, Elliot 131n. 12
eschatology 8, 11, 15, 117
ethical criticism 3, 21, 29–31, 37, 43, 46, 96, 121, 122, 128n. 9, 136n. 4
 see also didacticism
Evangelicalism 1–2, 32, 37, 75, 86, 106

fable 20, 43, 95
Farrar, F. W. 109
Ferguson, Fergus 77, 135n. 23
Fessler, Audrey 131n. 8
forgiveness 57, 85, 89
Fraser, Hilary 128n. 11
Frei, Hans 9, 124n. 17, 124n. 18
Friedman, Stanley 137n. 17
Fuchs, Ernst 125n. 22, 125n. 23
Funk, Robert 10–13, 17–19, 26, 125n. 22, 125n. 23, 127n. 2

Gallagher, Catherine 136n. 7
Gnosticism 35, 129n. 18
Goodlad, Lauren 106, 114
Govett, Robert 117, 137n. 10, 137n. 12
Gribble, Jennifer 94, 136n. 1, 136n. 5
Guthrie, Thomas 135n. 23

Ham, James Panton 94–5, 100
Hamilton, James 135n. 23
Hardy, Barbara 114
Harrison, Bernard 13–14, 77, 79
Hebrew scriptures 4–5, 19, 37, 123n. 7, 123n. 9, 124n. 16
Hedrick, Charles 13, 127n. 1, 138n. 21
Heilmann, Ann 134n. 12
Herzog, William 125n. 24
Hill, Nancy Klenk 94, 135n. 1, 138n. 20
hope 94, 96–7, 115–19
Hornbeck, Bert 94, 115
Horne, Brian 124n. 16
Horsley, Richard 129n. 16
Hurley, Robert 130n. 20
hypocrisy 51–2, 73, 132n. 15, 134n. 15

incarnation 32, 35–6
individual parables
 alert servants 100, 103–4
 ewe lamb 4–5, 98
 good Samaritan 6–8, 17, 20, 49, 95, 136n. 1
 Pharisee and publican 6, 17, 38, 42, 44, 47–61, 77–8
 pounds 100, 104, 111, 117, 125n. 24
 prodigal son 1–2, 6, 13, 19, 38–9, 63–91, 100–2, 113, 123n. 2, 126n. 24, 127n. 29
 rich fool 100, 102–3
 rich man and Lazarus 129n. 13
 talents 100, 103–4
 wheat and tares 116
 see also kingdom of God, limit-experience, New Hermeneutics, paradox, Paul Ricoeur
 wicked tenants 6

# INDEX

wise and foolish stewards 100, 103–4
workers in the vineyard 14
inheritance 57, 63, 86, 101, 107–8, 110
*see also* money, parables (prodigal son), stewardship

Jaffe, Audrey 99
Jager, Colin 128n. 11
Jasper, David 127n. 35, 128n. 11, 130n. 20
Jay, Elisabeth 74, 131n. 6, 132n. 1, 133n. 6, 133n. 10, 135n. 20, 135n. 25
Jeffrey, David Lyle 60
Jeremias, Joachim 8, 48, 123n. 6
Johnson, Maria Poggi 131n. 5
Jones, Geraint Vaughan 48
Joyce, James 17–18, 25
Juckett, Elizabeth 131n. 8
Judaism 4, 8, 14, 51, 124n. 10
*see also* Hebrew scriptures, midrash, parables (in Judaism)
Jülicher, D. Adolf 7–8, 11, 65

Kafka, Franz 16–17
Keble, John 42–3 47, 61
Kermode, Frank 17–19, 25–6, 28, 123n. 7
Kierkegaard, Søren 17
Kincaid, James 138n. 19, 138n. 25
kingdom of God 8, 10–11, 14, 25, 31, 37, 48, 59, 94, 115–17, 138n. 21
Kissinger, Warren 123n. 3, 124n. 14, 125n. 24
Knight, Mark 32, 128n. 11, 129n. 14
Knoepflmacher, U. C. 115
Kucich, John 94

Landow, George 129n. 19
Langbauer, Laurie 130n. 2
Langland, Elizabeth 134n. 11
Larsen, Timothy 32, 128n. 11
Larson, Janet 20, 94–7, 114
Leavis, Q. D. 131n. 3
Levine, Caroline 28–30, 36, 46, 59, 128n. 5–7
Levine, George 26, 33, 36–7, 107–8, 127n. 3, 128n. 4, 130n. 20, 136n. 7, 138n. 22
limit-experience 16, 24, 31, 33, 37, 44, 51, 57, 85, 88, 102, 119
Longenecker, Bruce 129n. 16
Loughlin, Gerard 124n. 16
Lovesey, Oliver 134n. 13, 134n. 17
Lowe, Brigid 128n. 9
Lukács, Georg 32–3

Maccoby, Hyam 124n. 12
Mason, Emma 32
McConnell, Frank 124n. 16
McFague TeSelle, Sallie 18–19, 125n. 24
McKelvy, William 128n. 11
metaphor 4, 12–13, 58, 125n. 19
Michell, Richard 137n. 11, 137n. 13
Michie, Elsie B 134n. 11
midrash 124n. 10
Milavec, Aaron 124n. 10
Miller, Andrew 29–30, 37, 46, 60, 131n. 10
Miller, J. Hillis 20, 25, 94, 114, 136n. 2
Mills, Kevin 19
Milton, Heather 134n. 11
Mintz, Alan 127n. 31
Mitchell, Rosemary 131n. 6
money 34–5, 40, 67, 100, 103–13, 129n. 16
capitalism 105

# INDEX

and Christianity  35
see also inheritance, stewardship
Morgan, Victoria  128n. 11
Moruzi, Kristine  131n. 8
Mundhenk, Rosemary  99

narrative reversal  5, 6, 24, 39–40, 44, 48, 50–1, 56, 85–8, 98–9
see also parable (defined), paradox
narrative theology  8–11, 124n. 16, 124n. 18
narratology  13, 15–16, 23
Naveh, Gila Safran  19
New Hermeneutics  10–11, 13–14, 18
Newey, Vincent  114
Newman, John Henry  46–7, 49, 60
Newton, Adam  128n. 8
Nissen, Johannes  130n. 20
Nord, Deborah Epstein  97

O'Connor, Flannery  17, 18
O'Mealy, Joseph  73, 134n. 11, 134n. 13
Oldenhage, Tania  127n. 30
Oliphant, Margaret  38–40, 63–91, 93, 122
  family life  42, 63–5, 69–70, 72, 83, 89, 91
  and gender  71
  moral views  73–4
  religious views  36, 66–7, 69–71, 83–4, 133n. 10, 134n. 15
  works,
    *Autobiography*  63–5, 69–70, 74, 79, 81, 83–4, 91, 133n. 8
    "Land of Suspense"  63, 89, 91
    "Open Door"  63, 68–9, 91
    *Perpetual Curate*  38, 63–5, 71–4, 78, 85, 90–1, 134n. 10, 13

*Who Was Lost and Is Found*  63, 67, 133n. 5
original sin  117
Oxford Movement  39, 42–3, 137n. 9

parables,
  allegorical exegesis  7, 14
  defined  4, 19, 24, 37
  etymology  98
  in Judaism  4, 124n. 10
  literary form of  8–12, 125n. 18
  in literature  15, 17–21
  and poststructuralism  11, 127n. 28
  and semiotics  125n. 24
  *Sitz im Leben*  8, 9
  Victorian exegesis  1–2, 49–50, 51, 77, 104–6
paradox  13, 15, 121
Parris, David  26
Paul (the Apostle)  51, 57–8, 129n. 16, 132n. 18, 132n. 19
Pereiro, James  131n. 9, 131n. 10
performativity  5, 11, 15–16, 20, 25, 30–1, 40
*peripeteia see* narrative reversal
Perkin, J. Russell  128n. 11
perlocutionary discourse  29–30, 40, 60
Perrin, Norman  124n. 24
Peterson, Linda  134n. 12
Pharisaism  40, 50–2, 61, 87–8, 132n. 13
Poland, Lynn  127n. 30
Polk, Timothy  123n. 9
Poovey, Mary  114
Prickett, Stephen  125n. 18
providential justice  65, 69, 71, 74, 76, 79–82, 84, 87–8, 118, 133n. 2
Punshon, W. Morley  135n. 23
Pusey, E. B.  49, 51, 55

Qualls, Barry  96, 114, 119

reader-response *see* perlocutionary discourse
realism  21, 23–4, 26–31, 42–3, 46, 58, 61, 88, 93, 96, 118, 128n. 6
  in parables  24–6
  and religion  31–2, 34–5, 37
Reed, John  99, 118, 135n. 23, 136n. 6
repentance  44, 54–61, 69, 75–7, 85, 88
reserve  40, 47, 80
resurrection  36, 117, 119
Ricoeur, Paul  12–16, 24–5, 27, 33, 48, 119, 121, 138n. 21
Riggs, Mike  20
Robbins, Jill  127n. 29
Robinson, Amy  134n. 11, 135n. 21
Robinson, Marilynne  17
Roman Catholicism  83
Romanes, Ethel  60, 132n. 16
Rubik, Margaret  68, 73–4, 133n. 5, 133n. 10, 134n. 15
Ruskin, John  28, 102

Sadrin, Anny  136n. 6
Sandbach-Dahlström, Catherine  43, 130n. 2
Sanders, Andrew  115, 136n. 2
Sanders, Valerie  134n. 12
Schaffer, Talia  44, 130n. 2, 131n. 8
Schaub, Melissa  134n. 12, 134n. 14, 134n. 19
Schipper, Jeremy  4, 123n. 7, 123n. 9
Scriven, Anne  134n. 12
secularity, secularism  31–6, 127n. 32, 129n. 12, 129n. 16
Seeley, Mary  137n. 13
self-knowledge  57, 98–9, 123n. 8

sermons  49, 55, 79, 81–2, 94–5, 135n. 24
Shakinovsky, Lynn  131n. 8
Shattock, Joanne  65, 72, 134n. 13
Shaw, Harry  26–8, 30, 36, 127n. 3, 128n. 5, 137n. 14
Shively, Steven  19
Sicher, Efraim  137n. 18
skepticism  28–31, 46, 49, 59, 99
Smith, Julianne  134n. 12
Smith, Karl Ashley  136n. 2
soteriology  2, 14
Spurgeon, Charles  77, 135n. 23
Stanley, Arthur Penrhyn  94–5, 100
Steiner, Lina  127n. 35
Stern, David  123n. 6, 124n. 10, 127n. 31
stewardship  100, 102–13, 117–19
  *see also* eschatology
Stirling, James  2, 105–6, 111, 137n. 11, 137n. 13
Stubbs, Charles  137n. 13
Styler, Rebecca  32, 129n. 15

Taylor, Charles  129n. 12
theology *see* atonement, conversion, eschatology, Gnosticism, hope, incarnation, kingdom of God, original sin, parables, providential justice, repentance, reserve, resurrection, soteriology, triumphalism, typology
Thoma, Clemens  123n. 7
Thompson, Nicola Diane  44
Thorne-Murphy, Leslee  131n. 8
Tolbert, Mary Ann  126n. 24
Tractarianism, *see* Oxford Movement
Trench, Richard Chenevix  50, 104, 135n. 23, 137n. 11

triumphalism 36, 118
Turner, Frank 31, 137n. 9
Turner, Mark 3
typology 37, 43, 131n. 6
 see also analogy

Via, Dan 9–10, 12, 124n. 11, 125n. 20
Victorian religious culture
 generally 21, 31–2, 128n. 11, 130n. 21
Viswanathan, Gauri 128n. 11

Wagner, Tamara 131n. 8
Wailes, Stephen 124n. 14
Wainwright, Valerie 128n. 8, 130n. 20
Walder, Dennis 136n. 2
Walker, Leila 134n. 18
Watt, Ian 26, 32–4
Wells-Cole, Catherine 132n. 17
Westbrook, Deanne 127n. 35
Wheatley, Kim 43, 130n. 2
Wheeler, Michael 96, 136n. 2
Wilder, Amos 26, 126n. 25, 126n. 26, 127n. 33

Williams, Clare 128n. 11
Williams, Isaac 47
Williams, Merryn 73, 132n. 1, 134n. 12, 134n. 13, 134n. 16
Witherington, Ben 129n. 16
Wolff, Robert Lee 59
Woodman, Thomas 128n. 11, 129n. 14
Wright, T. R. 124n. 16, 128n. 11

Yonge, Charlotte 37–40, 41–61, 91, 99–100, 122
 moral views 48–50, 54, 60–1
 theological views 47
 works,
  *Clever Woman of the Family* 43, 51–2
  *Heir of Redclyffe* 38, 42–61, 86, 99
  "Price of Blood" 41
Young, Brad 124n. 10

Zemka, Sue 128n. 11, 136n. 3

www.ingramcontent.com/pod-product-compliance
Lightning Source LLC
Chambersburg PA
CBHW052048300426
44117CB00012B/2032